A BORROWED LAND

Tinige' as
PETER R. ONEDERA

Published by University of Guam Press
Richard F. Taitano Micronesian Area Research Center (MARC)

303 University Drive, UOG Station
Mangilao, Guam 96923
(671) 735-2153/4
www.uogpress.com

ISBN: 978-1-961058-03-3 (hardback):
ISBN: 978-1-961058-02-6 (paperback)
ISBN: 978-1-961058-04-0 (library ebook)
ISBN: 978-1-961058-05-7 (trade ebook)
Library of Congress Control Number: 2024941160

Editor: Rindraty Celes Limtiaco
Copy Editor: Victoria-Lola Leon Guerrero

Cover and Interior Layout Designer: Ralph Eurich Patacsil
Cover Artist: Ralph Eurich Patacsil

A BORROWED LAND

Peter Onedera

UNIVERSITY OF GUAM
PRESS

I dedicate this book to my grandsons:

Tristen Ricardo
Matua Ånghet
Magåhet Judaiah
Maga'låhi Christopher
Mamau Yo'åse'
Uchan Sherrod
Adahi Sakieri

and my great grandson
Mason Jude

as well as my mother
Carmen Santos Onedera

This book waited for me, for decades, to finally get my act together and push for its completion and eventual publication.

I had internal emotions that wrestled at my very being, wrestling with whether to do it or not, whether I would be hurting others unintentionally, or whether I would be bringing up much anguish. I encountered many objections and hesitance in granting me interviews and shedding light on a difficult subject matter.

Indeed, it affected me mentally, emotionally, and physically, as much as I encountered when I first made an attempt to stage my full-act drama tragedy of *Ai Hagå-hu*, which was the true story of a CHamoru comfort woman.

The war years were a sensitive subject that was discussed only in print and broadcast media around the observance of the island's annual Liberation Day events. My work would be a major focus that stirred the minds, memories, and imagination of the local populace, and then it would disappear until the following year.

Today, in the 80th year of the island's liberation from Japanese invaders, this untold episode of the plight of the issei, nisei, and sansei of the century leading to World War II must be told.

For the first time ever, you will get a glimpse of what Guam was like through the eyes of this forgotten group that was never given a chance to share their stories.

I lahen-miyu as
si Peter R. Onedera

TABLE OF CONTENTS

PART 3

PART 4

FOREWORD

By Dr. Anne Perez Hattori

Peter Onedera's legacy already stands in posterity due to his hard-earned position as the leading CHamoru playwright of the 20th century. An exceptional resume of plays both written and performed cover important themes in our culture and history — of childhood memories, of World War II traumas, of the inhumane treatment of Guam's leprosy community, and more. He has also established his name as a CHamoru language activist, educator, and researcher, having served at the University of Guam as a professor of CHamoru language and as past director of the Kumision i Fino' CHamoru (CHamoru Language Commission). His publications include works detailing the history of Guam's village place names, as well as the first master's thesis written entirely in the CHamoru language.

Here, however, we see another dimension to Siñot Onedera — Peter as historian. This publication brings to the forefront a neglected yet important aspect of Guam's past as he bravely tackles the long and complex history of the island's Japanese community. His text spans the decades since the early 1900s, when Japanese men (and one woman) arrived on Guam, then intermarried and integrated into the local community, only to be cast aside as enemies-among-friends in the years before, during, and even after the war. Onedera began this research in 1987, so this publication brings into fruition decades of interviews with CHamoru persons of Japanese descent, many of whom have since passed on. Thus, this read tells a suppressed history from the voices of people themselves now silent except for their words that he brings to life.

Using a combination of oral interviews, archival sources, and family histories, Onedera's text balances his passion for storytelling and drama with his interest in honest depictions of a time that many might prefer to forget.

The decades before World War II receive the classical canonical treatment of Guam as a peaceful, idyllic island, but contemporary readers will gain great insight about a Guam that most were not yet born to experience. These were days before much of the farmlands had been confiscated by the military, a time in which people relied upon their ranches, the ocean, and the rivers for food. Thus, valuable lessons about subsistence living, about the *chenchule'* system of reciprocity, and about a general sense of community generosity and kindness resonate. But, once the war looms its ugly head, the romantic paradisical accounts get replaced by powerful, complex, and diverse stories of families caught in the middle of a war that had nothing to do with them.

While readers may be aware of World War II internment camps in the United States for Japanese-Americans living there, the story of Guam's Japanese community remains obscured — that is, until the publication of this ground-breaking volume. Indeed, the telling of World War II stories on Guam typically involves violent Japanese soldiers, victimized CHamoru villagers, and heroic American men. The standard telling of the War on Guam reduces our complex history to a simple story of good Americans and bad Japanese, with the valiant, homogenized CHamoru community struggling daily to survive. The fuller story told here includes complexities such as the reality of both CHamoru who collaborated with the Japanese, CHamoru innocently caught directly in crosshairs of the War, and Japanese-CHamoru on both sides of the fray. As Japanese who had married into CHamoru families in the early 1900s, and for the generations thereafter, as CHamoru with Japanese heritage, prior to the War, they had lived their lives entirely within the bounds of everyday CHamoru culture, speaking the indigenous language, practicing the native traditions, devoting themselves to the Catholic faith, and fishing and farming alongside the rest of the larger island community. Japanese married CHamoru and their CHamoru-Japanese children had all claimed Guam as their homeland. This publication tells that important pre-War story in richly detailed ways, capturing an era that no longer exists.

But its most powerful stories concerned the fractured relationships that resulted around the War. Questions about their identity, their loyalty, and their integrity emerge in ways never previously doubted among their fellow CHamoru. In this mayhem, they became doubly victimized in a war, not of their making — firstly, as CHamoru whose homeland had just been invaded, and secondly, as Japanese, whose allegiance was now at stake. Both their CHamoru neighbors and friends, and the invading Japanese forces placed pressures and expectations upon them, and how they responded forms the heart of this tale.

Peter Onedera shares his family story, but much more than that, our island's story. Although much has been written and said about World War II, precious little reflects the perspectives of a very uniquely situated group, the Japanese of Guam, who were made to feel that they lived on "borrowed land that you stole." Their resilience and adaptation to life in Guam, both during and after the war, make for compelling reading. This publication also reminds us that unattended wounds can fester, even 80 years later. And so, let the healing continue.

INTRODUCTION

By Rindraty Celes Limtiaco

Truth.

From a very young age, most of us are taught to speak and value the truth.

As we grow older, we realize that the truth isn't always comfortable. Maybe it's then that we learn to soften our truths when it might be too uncomfortable for those with whom we share.

In *A Borrowed Land*, these truths are not softened. Its author, Siñot Peter R. Onedera, shares these truths with uncompromising honesty.

Siñot Onedera has made it one of his life's missions to share the previously untold stories of our island's Nikkei — people of Japanese descent — before, during, and after World War II.

He spent years gathering information, stories, and truth from those who lived these experiences — not lived through, but lived these experiences. In his storytelling, Onedera clearly illustrates that there is a distinction between the two.

As a descendant of an issei, a first-generation immigrant, Onedera took on the responsibility of chronicling the Nikkei's experience on Guam — from their arrival to their assimilation into the island's life and culture, their hardship and resilience during the war, and what they endured after.

In his search for truth, Onedera discussed his difficulty in finding Nikkei survivors who were willing to tell their stories about how they were treated before, during, and after the war. He shared his emotional journey while listening to and recording their stories when they were finally ready to share. He opened up about his first-hand experiences with the discrimination that he and his family faced decades after the war had ended.

This book might make the reader uncomfortable.

Siñot Onedera tells the story of how Nikkei families were forced to isolate themselves before and during the war after they were shunned by their CHamoru relatives. He relays how they were forced to live in stockades after the war had ended, enduring heckling from their fellow Guamanians, including family members, for years afterward.

For many readers, what Onedera shares in his book will be revelatory. It is not something that is taught in school or in a Guam History class. They will be reading about these experiences for the first time.

Readers might wonder how these events could happen on an island where there is so much diversity and generosity shared between many different ethnicities and cultures. It may be difficult to know that the atrocities shared in this book are part of our truth.

But war is war. It is tragic. It is unmerciful. It brings out the best and the worst of humanity. And it seems our island was not spared.

Siñot Onedera deserves admiration for his work in bringing these stories and these truths to light. He has given voice to those who, for many decades, were silent. He is telling the stories of those who, for years, did not want to look back because of the pain, the trauma, and the hurt that they had endured. But in sharing these stories, he brings some form of closure, I believe, for the descendants of our island's issei.

More importantly, *A Borrowed Land* gives our island and our community the opportunity to learn from our past and hope that from these truths, something like this will never happen again.

"Hamyo ni' ManCHapanes mañåsaga hamyo gi iya Guam gi inayao tåno' ni' en sakke ha'."

"You Japs are all living on Guam on borrowed land that you stole."

PREFACE

I was born in the sleepy village of Sinahånña. I describe it as a sleepy village because that was how villages in the central part of the island were described. But what I remember was a bustling community and blocks of homes that stretched for miles, extending into the outskirts of CHa'ot, Åfa'me, Didige', Agana Springs, and to the Pipe Line, which is now Non-Title One of post-Urban Renewal. The village stretched to the campus of what was St. Jude Thaddeus School, now Bishop Baumgartner Memorial School, the previous convent of the Franciscan Sisters of Perpetual Adoration, and the Gaiety Theater that bordered Agana Heights. Along the main highway, there was Butler's and the Coca-Cola Bottling Plant, owned and managed by the Butler patriarch. Life in the village was alive with a very active Sinajana Civic Improvement Club.

I was born in June 1953, three years after President Harold S. Truman signed the Organic Act of Guam. I was the youngest of five. My four siblings were much older than me. My oldest brother had turned 18 when I came into the world. We didn't know each other as he joined the U.S. Army. Six years later, my second brother quit school in his junior year and somehow managed to enlist in the U.S. Navy. He was gone for much of my life growing up. My third brother died in infancy. My sister was 11 when I was born. By the time she entered high school, she'd gotten married and started her family.

My siblings and I all spoke CHamoru. I didn't fully learn English until I entered first grade at what was then Sinajana Elementary School and later became Carlos L. Taitano Elementary School. My mother, who was half CHamoru and half Japanese, spoke broken, poor English. She was adept in Japanese — enough to converse with her surviving siblings, Aunt Agueda and Uncle John. When I was a teen-ager, my mother and her siblings spoke Japanese when anything secretive was discussed. They didn't talk about these things in CHamoru as my siblings and cousins were all fluent. By the 1960s, most parents spoke in CHamoru if they didn't want their children to know what was being said. By then, English became the fascination, and everyone strived to be fluent in the language to survive in the burgeoning global community.

It was my mother and her siblings who taught me some of the Japanese words I knew, enough to comprehend but not converse. I didn't know until much later that there was such a thing as archaic Japanese. It was the language that my mother, Aunt Agueda, and Uncle John spoke when they were together. It wasn't the same language used by today's Japanese, as I came to learn much later when I worked for a moment as a hotel employee at the newly built Okura Hotel in Tomhom, which is now the Lotte Hotel Guam. Some of the words that I still remember are not in use anymore. I tried to pass them off to the Japanese tourists at the hotel. They didn't understand a thing I was saying.

My mother constantly used Japanese words intended to distinguish between different generations descended from an immigrant. The words and their meanings were later explained to me by Japanese friends. They are based on the numerical system that separates immigrants, their descendants, and relatives based on generations in their respective communities. These generational descriptors will be frequently referenced in nearly every chapter of this book. They figure significantly as they are relevant to the accounts that people shared with me.

I am part-Japanese and part CHamoru. I am a *sansei* (third-generation descendant of a Japanese immigrant). My *ojisan* (grandfather), who would be considered issei, came from Tochigi-ken, Japan, which is more than a two-hour train ride west of Tokyo. I learned the word Nikkei as an adult, but as a youngster, I was only familiar with nisei, which was a generational distinction, but also the name of the organization that my mother and her siblings were members of.

JAPANESE GENERATIONAL DESCRIPTORS

NIKKEI: Japanese immigrants and their descendants are known as Nikkei (pronounced KNEE-kay). In CHamoru, they were called *familian CHapanes* (Japanese families), descendants of the first Japanese patriarchs who came to Guam. Aside from assimilating into families through their marriage with local women, no other mention of a distinctive name was accorded to them other than the moniker *familian CHapanes*, except for one given to the Shimizu family known as *familian Kåcha*. To this day, many in the Nikkei community are often called *familian CHapanes* if an actual surname is not known.

ISSEI: The original Japanese citizens who came as immigrants are called issei (pronounced E-say). They are considered the first generation, having come to a place for the first time. They established domicile, became new citizens of their adopted homes, and lived there, usually for the rest of their lives. Legally, they weren't granted U.S. citizenship. In the early days of the U.S. Naval Government's rule on the island, these issei came to Guam by virtue of contract work on a copra plantation established by an issei named Jose Katsuji Shimizu. He was known as JK Shimizu and came by way of Saipan. JK Shimizu, also referred to as Shimizu-sama, will be mentioned throughout the book as he was highly respected by the Nikkei families since the start of the 20th century and into the war years. In my research, I could not find accounts of other issei who lived in Guam at the turn of the century, despite Saipan already having a burgeoning community of Japanese immigrants who were merchants or worked for the sugar plantation. JK Shimizu set up two copra plantations on Guam and was granted permission by Navy officials to hire annual contract workers from Japan. He is credited for bringing the influx of Japanese to the island and establishing the Nikkei community. Many Nikkei owe their connection to the island to JK Shimizu, who was later nicknamed Tåtan Kåcha. Allegiance and friendship were bestowed onto him by the men he hired and their families. Again, it was not known if there were other issei who came to Guam on their own. The earliest listing of *Japones* (the Spanish word for Japanese) lineage was from the 1920 Catholic church census.

NISEI: The children of issei who married local women are called nisei (pronounced KNEE-say). By the early 20th century many claimed mixed parentage that was comprised of Spanish, Filipino, German, Chinese, and American. The succeeding generation of a few women in these families also married issei men. When I was a youngster, I remember my family belonging to the Guam Nisei Association (GNA), which was an active non-profit group of the post-war and Organic Act era.

SANSEI: The grandchildren of issei are called sansei (pronounced SAN-say). Membership today in the GNA is mostly comprised of sansei. Current members include many prominent and active members of our civic and business community. I am also a sansei, although I've been an inactive non-paying dues member in the organization for several years now. My eldest cousin, Jiro', whom I interviewed and whose accounts are included in this book, was also a sansei. I relied upon him for the stories he shared that gave me further insight into the Nikkei community, but mostly for his memories of my grandfather and many relatives. Of note, Jiro', being the eldest of the grandchildren in our clan, was old enough to be my father as his first two sons were three and two years older than me, while his third child, a daughter, was a few months younger than me. This shows a difficulty among distinguishing nisei and sansei generations, which I refer to in another chapter. My grandfather referred to Jiro' as more of a nisei rather than a sansei as my grandparents had raised Jiro' since birth.

YONSEI: The great-grandchildren of the issei are called yonsei (pronounced YAWN-say). This would include my children and the children of the other members of the GNA.

These generation descriptors, while Japanese in meaning, aren't commonly used in Japan because they don't apply to the Japanese who did not immigrate to other countries. The terms applied only to those who immigrated overseas. For example, Brazil has about 1.5 million Japanese immigrants and descendants in their population. Hawai'i and the islands of the Pacific also have large populations of Nikkei.

Through Executive Order 9066, President Franklin D. Roosevelt established Japanese internment camps during World War II. From 1942 to 1945, the U.S. government made it a policy to incarcerate people of Japanese descent, despite being U.S. citizens, in what was referred to as isolated camps.

Historical accounts have shown Nikkei living in California, Arizona, Wyoming, Colorado, Utah, and Arkansas confined at internment camps during the war. On Guam, however, the issei, nisei, and sansei remembered all too clearly that the internment camps on island were called stockades by U.S. military officials. When the marines liberated the island, Japanese-CHamoru families were confined in the stockades AFTER the war.

There were also words and a.k.a. names used to ridicule and insult the Nikkei almost daily. People, mostly relatives, young and old, who stood outside the stockade in Tutuhan, now Agana Heights, shamelessly used these words, accompanied by obscenities. Many of the insults referred to physical deformities and appearances, ranging from *såtna* (visible sores on the body), *ke'yao* (walking with a limp), *pire'* (harelip), *patuleka* (bowlegged), *kitan* (cross-eyed), *lotsa* (lice infested), *båda* (female hunchback), *lao'an* (effeminate male), *nånu* (small in stature), *paladdang* (skin blister), *långnga'* (facial appearance of stupidity), *chatpa'go* (ugly), *repot* (stupor), *tåktamudu* (stupid), *debo'* (extremely obese), and *Jap* (a shortened word for Japanese that is derogatory).

And then there were the taunts and merciless teasing, which I wasn't spared from later in childhood. Japanese terms were used for these too, such as *kikkoman* (the bottled brand of the soy sauce), *daigo'* (Japanese radish also called daikon), *miso* (the paste used for the soup ingredient), and *sasime'* (fresh tuna cut into slices smothered with mashed wasabi with lemon and soy sauce). Other taunts included *bachigo'* (slanted eyes) and *chingching* (pinched eyelids).

My surname was ridiculously re-pronounced as *ponedera* to reflect that of the "*hen*," in animal husbandry. Elderly Nikkei were not referred to with the respectful use of "Tan" or "Tun."

TERMINOLOGIES

In the Spanish era, the early 1900s and up to the war years, the words "Tan" and "Nan" were used in spoken CHamoru as honorific terms for men and women who were respected as elders or the elderly, with the latter term referring to biological age. It accompanied first and nicknames of individuals when addressing them with the gesture of the sniffing of the hands or *mannginge'*.

A man, single, married, or widowed was called Tan Enrique, Tan Ramon, Tan Clemente, and Tan CHu' for Tan Jesus. This is not to be confused with the Tan now accorded to females. Tan for males was a shortened, if not, abbreviated form of "Tåta" and because the CHamoru was a close-knit community, discipline was also meted out by older males who could be the patriarch of the family next door or in the neighborhood, an uncle, grandfather, godfather, older cousin, or someone of authority. Therefore, Tåta with the addition of the consonant "n" used with a first name or nickname was meant to be Tåtan Enrique, Tåtan Ramon, Tåtan Clemente, and Tåtan CHu' which deviated to Tan and was in place with speakers up until the war years.

Females were referred to as Nan Li'a', Nan Metsedes, Nan Juliana, and Nan Marikita, which, like Tåta, actually meant Nånan Li'a', Nånan Metsedes, Nånan Juliana, and Nånan Marikita. Most of the individuals I interviewed interchanged these honorific terms through many of our conversations and their accounts. The Tan and Nan distinction also included the Spanish-speaking terms of Don and Doña, but Doña did not catch on in popular usage. Don did, such as with Don Pedro Martinez of Hagåtña. Don Pedro somehow retained the honorific as he was also well-connected to the Catholic church, but for those who weren't Catholics, he was also called Tun Pedro Martinez.

Somehow, the post-war era ushered in the popular use of English, which then fostered gender distinction, and Tun came about, and that inadvertently included the Don of Spanish-era use. So, I've used Tun in reference to the war years of accounts by many of the issei, nisei, and sansei men as well as Tan for reference to the females. Today, these honorifics are used interchangeably, and, I, for one, can readily tell when a person uses the terms I've described here; I most certainly can tell which era they represent or are familiar with. Hence, in succeeding chapters of this book, I use "Tan," as well as "Tun," in reference to males and "Tan" in reference to females.

I use the word CHamoru as both a singular and plural noun, similar to how I use the work Nikkei. I wanted to supplant this as a frame of reference. I avoided the word "CHamorus" as modern speakers tend to pluralize CHamoru words with the addition of the English letter "s" such as in "todu" becoming "todus." "CHamoru siha," could also be the plural for CHamoru, but "siha," also has a personal plural pronoun meaning, "They are CHamoru." I want the reader to be familiar with this usage. Other words that will be used as both singular and plural nouns include CHapanes, Refalawasch, CHinu, and other ethnicities that might be referred to in the book. I hyphenated those with mixed parentage such as CHamoru-CHapanes.

Many of the accounts in this book may be difficult to ascertain, and there will be questions of accuracy and truth. I took into account all that was shared by those I interviewed. I never questioned their veracity as they spoke with conviction from first-hand experiences, which I respected and took to heart. Some, too, may be difficult to prove factual, but the gist I shared was something that I saw in their eyes, heard in their voices, and felt in their emotions.

I must give credit to Tony Palomo's writing of *An Island in Agony*. I read that book more than once. There were passages of accounts about some of the issei and nisei. It was the only book that shed light on the community of Nikkei in the days of the pre-invasion and the invasion itself. I consider that book to be the only indication that there was something more to the plight of these people during the island's darkest days. I truly felt there wasn't enough. As a sansei, having had the opportunity to speak with some of the manåmko' (elderly) issei, nisei, and sansei, there was a sense of urgency in me that told me that there was another side to the World War II indignities and suffering.

All the people that I spoke to prior to the writing of this book inspired me to give them their moments to share. I felt "faith in God gives meaning and purpose to human life," a first line in a creed of my involvement in the Latte Jaycees. Through their storytelling, I felt their renewed hope, the almighty father in Heaven, Sånta Marian Kåmalin, allegiance to Old Glory despite being of mixed emotions to their country of origin, but also to their newfound land, and a fervent belief that World War II wouldn't be forever.

PART ONE

CHAPTER 1
Talk Story

My mother told me that I was a sansei. I was six years old. This happened late one afternoon after I had played with the neighborhood kids. Our choice of play back then was the re-enactment of war, the battle between the American troops and the Japanese soldiers. All over the island, children considered playing war a highlight of those post-war years, as the emphasis on the Japanese occupation and eventual defeat was to drive home the point that the country of Japan lost to the Americans. The locals praised the U.S. victory daily. It extended into the early '60s when the fervor of U.S. loyalty was at its height.

As in all things, when playing war, no one wanted to be the enemy. Those who managed to have U.S. Marines' helmets always took the top role of playing the soldiers. Whoever was a chum to someone on the American team would also end up being a member of the U.S. squadron of kids. Those considered unfit to be an American soldier ended up with the Japanese troops. Either way, our war game consisted of an even number of soldiers for both sides. We then played joyfully, always loudly mouthing the words, "pow, pow, pow," or "bang, bang, bang" with cut branches of *tångantångan* (invasive wood grown after the war to curb erosion) that we chose as our make-believe rifles. Of course, wearing the helmet was an added bonus to the make-believe battle.

That afternoon, it was dusk. My mother and I were in our living room. I had showered, changed into *bahåkke* (non-dressy, casual attire for home or yard wear), and obediently sat before my mother. She appeared serious. It was right before we were to eat an early dinner.¬¬ She then started to tell her story, which had details I had never known. I was mesmerized, and it was the beginning of my fascination for "talk story."

My mother explained our Japanese heritage. There were details about families of Japanese descent whom she identified as either issei, nisei, or sansei. She said her father, Zenpei Jito, an issei, came from a place called Tochigi somewhere near Tokyo. He came to Guam, worked for a time, then met and married my grandmother, Nånan Li'a' (Maria). My mother, Måme' (Carmen), was the firstborn; followed by Auntie Maikita (Maria); then Auntie Nena' (Ana); Uncle John, her brother, whose baptized name was Juan; and the youngest was Auntie Då (Agueda). My mother and her siblings were the nisei. My siblings, cousins, and I comprised the sansei generation.

I was full of questions. I was fascinated and pressed for more, conjuring pictures in my mind while she spoke of those years of her life. She was born in 1913. As the eldest, she was a formidable part of the family as she had to help maintain the household and rear her siblings while doing the obligatory tasks expected of the eldest child. I'd listen spellbound to her tales of relations near and far; of her strict upbringing; of fishing, planting, and seasonal harvests; of Guam as it developed from tiny hamlets into expanded villages; of ranches in village outskirts and deep jungles; and of small infrastructure improvements.

There were many other details. I began looking forward to hearing her stories. I'd see that she, too, was captivated as she eagerly spoke of her youth, but there were dark shadows that brought tears and a look of fear, and then she'd stop. I remember plying her with questions about the war, of torture and death, as I'd heard from snatches of conversations by adults in the neighborhood. She'd skip those details. I would soon realize that she didn't readily touch upon her ordeals during the war. She left that part of her stories untold until she was more settled and composed.

Late at night as I'd walk on her back, to massage her before she fell asleep, she'd continue with stories that included names of people, some long gone; of places that I couldn't relate to or weren't on any familiar map and of activities that included play, work, and good-natured moments of sharing and camaraderie with relatives or friends. However, the period of the Japanese occupation was fraught with fear, worry, hunger, sickness, torture, death, betrayal, caution, self-exile of families, the lack of receiving church sacraments, and prayers at all hours of the day and night. She mentioned, too, the tremendous distrust shown to her and other Nikkei by former neighbors, maternal relatives, colleagues, godsiblings, and even village leaders like the commissioner, *pattera siha* (mid-wives), teachers, *techa siha* (church prayer leaders), and *suruhåna siha* (herbal healers).

My mother also spoke of kindness, giving, helping one another through moments of hardship, and grieving for the loss of loved ones. She said, though, that the good deeds that did occur were often isolated and kept within trusted networks. The CHamoru priests Oscar Calvo and Jesus Baza Duenas rendered kindness and bestowed blessings, communion, and Mass whenever allowed by Japanese officials. Confessions were plentiful, held in secret in homes as churches were practically deserted because they were closely watched.

By 1960, as I approached age 7, I was more alert and aware of my environment. I wondered about the middle-aged man from the village who would walk down the block, stand in front of my house, and scream obscenities to no one in particular. I'd kept myself hidden in the house. Our front door, like most homes in those days, was covered by a colorful curtain from the yardage sold at Butler's. Many homes were like that.

That man would cuss, scream, and shout in a drunken rage telling us in CHamoru, "Hamyo ni' ManCHapanes mañåsaga hamyo gi iya Guam gi inayao tåno' ni' en sakke ha'." This translated to "You Japs are all living on Guam on borrowed land that you stole." I remember his exact words to this day. He'd conclude with: "I want you all to disappear or die in agony."

In his tirade, the man would pick up rocks in the yard and hurl them through the curtain into the living room. There was some civility in his manner as he never hurled those rocks through our louvered glass windows. After he finished, I would watch him saunter up the block until I couldn't make him out. I would then sweep the rocks from the living room and into the yard where I knew he'd grab them again the next time he came by.

I never knew him, but my mother was aware of him. All she'd tell me was, "Never mind, my son, just show him respect if you ever see him." I learned later that he had witnessed the beheadings of his immediate family, which included his parents, grandparents, and siblings, and had a difficult time during the war. I believe he turned to alcohol to relieve himself of the painful memories.

Other times, I'd overhear older cousins talk about being beaten by bullies at school, at village stores, at sodality (organization of teenage girls assigned for church maintenance, cleaning, and upkeep) gatherings at the parish church or *eskuelan påle' siha* (parochial schools), just because they had slanted eyes or because they were known to be part Japanese. They'd say that they were often mocked and ridiculed or were subjected to merciless pranks and trickery. I'd see my female cousins burst into tears while my male cousins just gritted their teeth. They'd all say that the neighborhood bullies who mistreated them weren't to be trusted and so, they kept their distance.

Some elderly people were disrespected by children and young adults because their parents told them not to bother with the customary kissing of the hand because of the elderly's Japanese lineage or as women who married issei.

At night, too, marauding kids or teenagers would throw rocks on top of our tin-roofed house. It created quite a disturbance that must have awoken nearby households. Our house was the only one on the block that received this treatment. My grandmother, who has long since died, and my mother and her youngest sister, who continued living with us, learned early on not to respond. Although it happened often, it stopped when there was no response from our household.

Among adults, post-war humiliation warranted unemployment by private companies and even the government. Those with Japanese surnames didn't get as far as interviews. Surnames such as Iwatsu, Haniu, Miyasaki, Okada, Murakami, Yoshida, Sugiyama, Takano, and others weren't considered worthy of hiring. Many of the people I interviewed shared aspects of social angst, some based on the experiences of their parents and siblings. In the churches, some parishes didn't permit *techa siha* (prayer leaders) who were of Japanese lineage to recite prayers for annual festal patrons or for the nine nights of a rosary for the deceased in private homes. They also remembered non-inclusion at PTA functions and political pocket meetings, and denial of consideration for sports teams in softball and for some government services. Once, a post-war mom-and-pop store owned by a CHamoru man and his wife refused patronage to a nisei family for the purchase of essentials like milk, eggs, and canned goods.

In my childhood, I often gasped in shock as my mother related stories that I felt were perhaps cruel. She made me understand that war was war, and the true colors of people are often brought to the forefront because of ignorance and fear, often spurred by petty gossip drawn from suspicion and other evil thoughts. It would leave me wondering for days why cruelty seemed to abound during times of civil strife and war. This was still a foreign experience or ordeal that I didn't understand. I could not imagine it.

CHAPTER 2
Early Years

Our family history centered upon my grandfather, Zenpei Jito Onodera. He perished toward the end of the war, and his fate continues to be a family mystery. Although I didn't know him, older cousins who grew up before the war knew and remembered him. He was a tall man, they said. My cousins spoke about how he'd become such a devotee to his adopted Catholic faith, and that he'd spoken CHamoru fluently, but had a speech challenge. He had trouble pronouncing words that used the English letter "J" like in Jell-O, jar, and jacket, instead saying **th**ello, **th**ar, and **th**acket; and with the letter "L," it was pronounced as an "R:" Jell-O became **th**ero, leaf became **r**eaf, and location became **r**ocation. He was *"paya',"* (having a speech impediment). He never spoke the English language.

My grandmother, Nånan Li'a', hailed from the CHetton-Balitres clan whose origins were from Tomhom. The early years of their marriage began in that hamlet even while my grandfather worked on a copra plantation. The first three offspring, all girls, were born in Tomhom. My grandfather worked most of his life for the copra plantation owned and run by Jose Katsui Shimizu. My grandfather was close to him. Many of the issei JK Shimizu brought over from Japan, including my grandfather, called him Tåtan Kacha. JK Shimizu was regarded with respect. There was a universal sentiment that he was the patriarch of the Nikkei community.

I questioned relatives who knew my grandfather. Our family referred to our grandfather as **Tåtan Dera'**. That was how we addressed him despite many of his grandchildren never having met him. To learn about him, I spoke at great length with older cousins, as well as former elderly neighbors and the few issei who knew and worked with him at the copra plantation. Tåtan Dera' assimilated into the community after he decided that Guam was home. He never returned to Japan. He chose to stay here, married my grandmother, eventually managed the copra plantation, and learned everything he could about the island, the culture, and the dominant religion. He had a small soda fountain in Hagåtña that was managed by my grandmother. Together they raised five children who became the nisei generation.

My grandfather is an integral part of this story, although his representation is, for the most part, a literary re-enactment, pieced together based on the information I could gather about him. If he were alive today, I know that I would have loved and cherished him for, overall, it was said that he was respectful, kind, and generous.

From my mother's stories, I learned that Tåtan Dera' taught all his children to speak Japanese. Although baptized in the Catholic faith and given Christian names, he also gave the first few grandchildren Japanese nicknames. Some names that continued into adulthood included my sister Maria, who became known as Mariko'; and the eldest grandson whom he reared, Jose, became known as Jiro'. I interviewed Jiro' and included his accounts in this book. While I don't know the Japanese meaning of Mariko', I assumed that it must be the English equivalent of Maria. Jiro' means "the second son," as he was given the name because he was raised by Nåna and Tåtan Dera'. My grandfather's only son was Uncle John, who, like his sisters, didn't get Japanese nicknames. In adulthood, Jiro' owned the Onedera Store in Dededo for more than 50 years. Other names my grandfather gave to older grandchildren were Saburo (my brother Augusto), Shiro (my brother Jose), and Hachiko' (my eldest female cousin Anita), who died in childhood.

I had never met or spoke to my grandfather as he perished during the war, and his remains were never found. He was never given proper burial rites.

My grandmother, known to relatives and neighbors as Nan Li'a', also died and was never given the customary burial accommodations befitting a widow. I was only three years old when she passed away. My mother told me that my grandmother babysat me while my mother went to work and my siblings were off to school. My Auntie Då was also married and began her family in the late '50s and early '60s.

My mother's childhood consisted of memories of Tomhom. The CHetton clan lived in harmony. Sustenance was a key factor in their lives. My mother and her siblings learned about fishing and harvesting from the waters and shores of the bay. Nearly every family living there knew the various methods of fishing that included the *gadi* (night fishing with long nets), *tekken* (gill nets), *talåya* (circular throw nets), *eguihan* (capturing fish), *etupak* (bottom line fishing), *pisao* (pole fishing), *etokcha'* (spear fishing), *edipok* (line fishing in a water hole near the reef), and *lumulai* (moonlit night fishing with a pole and a line). Everyone knew the harvesting seasons and the phases of the moon as they related to the harvests. Boys and girls were adept at all methods of fishing, which also included catching octopi, cat-eye shells, clams in the sand at low tide, the edible seaweed called *addo'* that was harvested on the reef, and the favorite ingredients of seafood chowder in coconut milk with the favored *dukduk siha* (small hermit crabs). During certain seasons, families would line the shores with nets in hand to catch *mañåhak* (juvenile rabbit fish), *ti'ao* (goat fish), and *atulai* (big eye scad).

Equally, too, families were just as adept at river fishing as *asuli* (freshwater eels), *ito'* (catfish), *tilåpia* (fresh water fish), and *uhang* (shrimp) added sustenance to the meal tables. In the jungles, moonlit catches of *pånglao siha* (land crabs) and *ayuyu* (coconut crabs), in addition to the capture of *fanihi siha* (fruit bats), *binådu* (deer), and *babuen hålom tåno'* (wild pig), provided much sought after dishes.

On the land, planting and harvesting included *mai'es* (corn), varieties of lemon, *pipinu* (cucumber), *birenghenas* (eggplant), *tumåtes* (tomatoes), okra, *kangkong* (water spinach), *atmagosu* (bitter melon), and root crops such as *suni* (taro), *gaddo'* (wild yams), *dågu* (regular yams), *kamuti* (sweet potato), and *mendioka* (cassava). Fruits that also commanded seasons but took years to mature and ripen included *lemmai* (breadfruit), *mångga* (mango), *alageta* (avocado), *åtes* (sweet sop), *anonas* (custard apple), *laguanå* (soursop), *lāngka'* (jackfruit), *chandiha* (water melon), and *kalamasa* (pumpkin).

People who grew up on the island, knew the local names and descriptions of the harvests from the sea, as well as from the rivers and the land. A CHamoru who did not know the names, descriptions, and seasons would bring on familial shame. Japanese forces sought out these harvests for the feeding of Japanese soldiers and officials during the war years. Many families had harvests forcefully taken from them, bringing near starvation to the populace as they were pillaged repeatedly.

My mother and her siblings learned how to survive and provide sustenance from the ocean and their labors on land. In addition to tasks required of their gender, they learned housework, yardwork, fishing in rivers and the sea, planting, hunting in the jungles for wild animals, and preparing daily meals — morning, noon, and night. All tasks were mastered by children in CHamoru households by the time they reached age 10. It was rare to hear of laziness, slovenly ways, and being idle, as consequences were often meted out in physical punishment such as the *kuåtta* (a whip made from dried cow's tail used for spanking). There was no such thing as "time outs" and "restrictions."

In pre-war years between 1915 and 1930, there was peace and tranquility. Anyone who had a relationship with relatives, friends, and neighbors knew of trust, generosity, kinship, sharing, and lending a helping hand.

More than a hundred years have passed since the beginnings of the Nikkei community on the island — more than a hundred years' worth of stories waiting to be told. Sometimes stories stay buried because it's not their time to come forth. Often, there needs to be time to heal before we are ready to face truths. In this case, we have the gift of a hundred years of luxury of life that Guam accorded to the island's populace, be they CHamoru or mestison CHapanes.

CHAPTER 3
A Class Assignment

In the spring semester of 1987, a University of Guam class assignment allowed me the opportunity to delve further into my Japanese background. I was assigned to interview members of the issei, nisei, and sansei families who were by then fully entrenched in the community in their various villages.

It was a daunting task as my goal was to meet at least 20-to-30 individuals, most of whom were retirees and elderly, who had first-hand accounts of life on the island during the war years. Aside from common names that I was familiar with, based on just personal knowledge and those shared by countless friends and relatives, I could only rely on word-of-mouth connections. My only asset, I felt, was that I spoke fluent CHamoru and that my surname would spark recognition of my family heritage, allowing possible interviewees to be comfortable with me.

It was discouraging, at first, as many simply refused to recount painful memories of the war. Initially, there were five issei, many others were nisei and sansei. I was even scolded by three issei who felt I had no business inquiring about the war years, even after they had learned that I was a descendant. They felt that seeking responses to questions about things I did not experience was none of my business. From those five issei, only one was willing to be interviewed. Two died not long after our initial conversations, and I lost track of the other two. Some nisei had health challenges, and one died of natural causes after I initiated telephone contact. Others varied from nisei to older sansei who were willing but cited difficulties in transportation or their home environment. Four sansei were still gainfully employed and couldn't accommodate juggling work schedules.

That semester was a tremendous challenge. I was able to secure interviews with my first and only issei, Tun Takayoshi "Jose" Okamitsu, an elderly but spritely man who could speak in both English and CHamoru as well as Japanese. He turned out to be one of two individuals that I was able to talk to, but it was the second interviewee, a nisei woman, Tan Katalina Maiyami, who provided profound information that made me thirst for more. She shared a part of the island's history that I had never read about in news accounts or in media coverage during the annual July Liberation Day celebrations. Her interview spurred me to look for more.

For that spring semester, because I had yet to reach the desired number of credible interviewees for my assignment, I earned an incomplete grade. However I consulted with the professor and asked to be allowed to continue the project into the summer and fall semesters. She granted me the opportunity, which allowed me to make significant progress.

This nisei woman was a tremendous help. She contacted others, and with her encouragement and support, I was able to meet and interview more people. During that summer's Liberation Day festivities, there were memorial services. I went to the Tinta' and Fåha' sites in Malesso. I didn't know that the massacres of their village leaders had been a yearly observance dutifully attended by the village. A dedicated commissioner, who by law was elevated to the role of mayor through a legislative act, spearheaded the observance.

I also attended a memorial service in Assan, held at the parish church. The nisei woman, whom I first interviewed, accompanied me. Before the religious services began in the Niñu Perdido Church, she introduced me to three people, two who were nisei and another, who was a sansei. I was able to schedule meetings with them at their homes. They were not related, but were close acquaintances through their lineage as well as in their social lives. Other memorials that now occur annually in CHagui'an, Asinan, Tå'i, Mangilao, Sumai, Fenna, and Manenggon weren't observed yet.

I based my initial questions for these new interviewees on the information that I gleaned from the only issei and the first nisei and sansei that I had interviewed. With these three individuals, I began to realize how their lives had been changed during the war. I took copious notes in the spiral notebooks I brought along. I recorded their responses on a hand-held recorder that used mini-cassette tapes, while simultaneously writing profusely. I had neglected to photograph them, but that was because I couldn't afford a decent camera. I met the three individuals about three more times. True to my assessment, I used my fluent CHamoru to tailor and plan my questions, and I listened several times to the recorded information while re-reading the notes I took. I began formulating additional questions that I'd maneuvered into the next set of interviews I conducted.

By the beginning of the next semester, I acquired four additional interviews. My perspective of the Nikkei community's survival during the war years began taking shape. This time, I softened my approach, and my questions were asked with greater caution, as I began encountering a mix of emotions from the interviewees. There was anger, despair, even loneliness, many tearful disclosures, and a feeling of betrayal that many of them couldn't shake off. They were subjected to atrocities by relatives, usually from their mother's side, especially when they themselves were nisei. Their mothers had married Japanese nationals, the issei of that historical period of the island.

I listened. I learned patience. At times, I was moved, but I had to learn to control and keep my emotions in check. I asked questions, recorded responses, and furiously jotted important information such as names, places, ages, and often, the connection of a.k.a. names inherited from CHamoru mothers or grandmothers who married Japanese men. I accumulated a stack of spiral notebooks, in addition to the mini-cassettes that I would listen to many times after an interview, to make sure that everything was clear to me. Fortunately, all of them allowed me to call them and re-visit accounts that I needed clarified.

I was also invited to *fi'esta* gatherings, barbecues, and joyous occasions, such as weddings and christenings — a university graduation, a retirement party, and a 50th golden wedding jubilee. I was invited to celebrate with another family whose relative, a nun, was celebrating her years in the convent. I became friends with many family members, many of whom were of my generation. I lost track of whether they were sansei, perhaps yonsei, too.

I completed the assignment in the fall semester with my 15-page research paper successfully submitted to my professor. I earned an "A" grade and was satisfied that I had fulfilled my obligation.

In the end, I interviewed 14 people, one of whom was an issei, the 13 others were descendants, either nisei or sansei but none beyond that. They were not related to each other by marriage or blood, except for a brother and a sister who lived next door to each other on the northern outskirts of a village.

My first cousins, my brother, relatives, neighbors and others I'd met with, who were born before the war, provided additional knowledge. I didn't include them in the count of actual Nikkei I interviewed, but they are included in the acknowledgement page, along with others I've met and spoken with through the years.

With an intense inquisitiveness about the generations that originated the Nikkei, I plied people with ceaseless questions. I considered their stories of tremendous value, and I added them to what I had already learned from my mother, my aunt, and my grand-aunt who have all passed away.

CHAPTER 4

A Lost Period, Untold Stories

Despite fulfilling the obligatory assignment of that university year, my life took on new challenges. Work, marriage, fatherhood, diabetes, and many other activities took precedence. I set aside the interviews, and they laid dormant for decades. From time to time, I'd pull my work out of oblivion, glance, reread, rewrite, and add anecdotes from new information I'd gleaned at chance meetings with others who were sansei or succeeding generations; as well as some who shared stories about their in-laws and what they knew of their family's histories. The mini-cassettes started deteriorating in quality, as new modes of media began surfacing and replacing old ones that became obsolete.

Until now.

I brought the notes and recordings out from storage. I began rewriting my decades-old submission to my college professor. I ironed out grammar, sentence structure, and spelling. I corrected the identities of those who responded to the interviews and added CHamoru glossaries with Japanese terms that I remembered. I listened to the few mini-cassettes that could still be played on a borrowed old mini-cassette recorder and re-read those copious notes from the spiral notebooks that hadn't yellowed. I was able to piece together important information that I had painstakingly wrote. It became another labor of love.

I must interject here that I also started attending rosaries and funerals for some of those I had interviewed. In one year, in the late 1980s, I recall attending funerals for three of the elderly people I had interviewed. Today, many, if not all, perhaps, of the nisei and some sansei have passed away. The only issei who provided much-needed start-up information about other issei was gone now, too, from this earth. I wanted to tell their stories. Their stories weren't told.

This book is about them. Out of deference, I listed their names on the acknowledgment page, but I didn't identify them with their accounts in this book. I gave them fictitious names. While they shared their stories, I was in awe of their resilience and their ability to recount moments of sheer agony and grief, but what captured me most was their physical reactions as they shared their genuine experiences and recollections.

It must be noted that the Nikkei families had different experiences. It would be unfair to compare their treatment, mistreatment, lifestyle, and per-spectives of the war years. Some of the respondents gave heart-wrenching ren-ditions of atrocities, humiliating submissions to the demands of the Japanese officials, and betrayal by CHamoru relatives. Others spoke of being deprived of their livelihoods with the pillaging of goods, provisions, and livestock. Still others were subjected to being maids, housekeepers, yard keepers, and bar-racks and lavatory custodians. There were also those who had to cook, do laundry, build and furnish facilities, and bathe Japanese officers.

There were countless demands made on many Nikkei families. Some isolated stories included favored treatment of some families, as well as being provided with niceties that included food, refreshments, and special services. The Japanese rice wine or sake was a favored *presento'* (gift) that was relished by local families. But no one was spared a moment by the Japanese military, for, after all, they were still Japanese despite being of the lowest rank of social standing as noted by the conquerors. A half-cast or a watered-down second or third generation descendant was looked down upon by the Japanese invad-ers. Most of the local Nikkei population wasn't trusted and was cast aside as unworthy of time and attention, only as subjects to do the conquerors' bidding.

As decades passed, while my work lay idle, other paths in my life opened up, too. This included my work as a playwright. One significant period of that work involved meeting, by chance, a CHamoru woman who laid bare her ordeals of being forced into the life of a comfort woman. The countless hours of interviews and the stories she told, shook my very being as, indeed, man's inhumanity to man, was told to me through the eyes of that woman. It was another aspect of life during the war years where I had to ponder in disbelief. I experienced nightmares. From that woman's stories, I presented the play titled *Ai Hagå-hu (Oh, my Daughter)* to packed audiences at the University of Guam Fine Arts Theater for two weeks in March 1997. From that showing, I was contacted by people —CHamoru and a few other nisei and a couple of sansei — who wanted to share their stories. I included their stories in some of the chapters here. They, too, added new dimensions to the stories I had collected.

Then, from 2012 to 2016, I moved to San Diego, California to, as others would laugh at my disclosure, "have bragging rights that I'm a *CHamoron san-lagu* (stateside CHamoru)" because that city alone boasts the largest concentration of CHamoru expatriates in the continental United States, as supported by Michael Lujan Bevacqua, in an April 2016 article, where he wrote about the Chamorro Diaspora, noting that San Diego is the area with the largest diasporic Chamorro population that he called *'ma'gas na sinahi,'*. The fact was supported by the 2000 census.

I knew several people in San Diego who were former Sinajana, Kañåda, Dededo, and Tamuning residents, or who were former elementary, junior high, high school, and university classmates, as well as previous colleagues in the various jobs that I have held throughout the years. I even joined the Sons and Daughters of Guam Club of San Diego and served briefly as its secretary and a member of the board of directors.

From that period in San Diego, I had met several nisei and sansei, some of whom knew my family. A woman, whom I'll call Nan Pai', introduced herself to me during a reception of the Saint Francis novena and Mass at the clubhouse on James Jones Avenue. She said my mother was her godmother and she knew her quite well. She told me she attended my mother's wake and funeral. I didn't know her, but she knew me and my siblings. She was originally from Pago Bay and was born in 1933. She said she was about 10 years old when her parents tasked her to visit my mother and family at Tokcha', where they were living at the then-abandoned copra plantation. She was to deliver a store-bought, 10-pound sack of *mai'es arina* (corn flour) and *asiento*, a form of starch used for stiffening clothes while ironing. Walking through the jungles from Pago Bay to Tokcha', she could hide in verdant vegetation should she come across marauding Japanese soldiers.

She said she never forgot the horror she witnessed as my mother, Auntie Då, and my grandfather handed their gunny sack of food and vegetables that came from their meager garden to Japanese soldiers. All three were kneeling in abject obedience as two soldiers stood brandishing their bayonets, with a third harshly talking to them. The soldier was cursing and using Japanese vulgarity. It dawned on Nan Pai' that my family would be beheaded, which was why they were kneeling. Nan Pai' said none of them spoke. She said she silently prayed as she crouched, hidden in a bushy shrub. She feared for Ninan Måme' (Godmother Carmen) and Auntie Då, while it seemed that Tåtan Dera was ready to meet his fate with his head bowed. Then a distant shout from another soldier diverted the three soldiers' attention, and they left the interrogation. Tåtan Dera, my mother, and Auntie Då collapsed to the ground sobbing. Nan Pai', possibly in her late 70s, was trembling as she shared her story.

My mother never told me about that ordeal, but I think that must have been one of those times, during her storytelling, when she balked at going further into detail.

CHAPTER 5

Some Commonalities

During my interviews, all respondents shared some common information. The first was that the Nikkei kept to themselves and didn't live among the clusters of community that included relatives and former neighbors. When the news of pending war began circulating a year before the invasion, they believed that neighbors and maternal relatives began treating them differently. They were ignored, shunned from social activities like celebrations and festive occasions, and kept at a distance. Parents of daughters who had married Japanese men ignored them. Not long after, it spread to aunts, uncles, and distant elders. Soon, they were no longer included in patron saint novenas and the rites of sacrament at the church that included baptisms, communions, confirmations, and marriages. A Nikkei family was chased out of a pre-marital *komplimento*, (an evening reception at a bride-to-be's home before the morning church nuptial) by the bride-to-be's mother.

Gossip and innuendo soon took hold of the local populace. Whispers started about possible traitor-like behavior of issei, although many had no idea of who the impending invaders would be. Treatment by *suruhåna siha* (herbal healers) stopped altogether; *pattera siha* (mid-wives) refused assistance to birthing mothers; anniversary death rosaries, wakes, and funerals became devoid of neighbors and relatives. Many Nikkei were emotionally pained and began to keep to themselves. They found self-exile in remote jungle areas and away from the community. They soon felt that they were people without a country. They believed that the rest of the community was not concerned about their well-being, as they struggled to survive and maintain normalcy among their families. The wives were the most hurt. They watched in anguish as their Japanese husbands, children, and grandchildren were mistreated and shunned by most everyone.

Anyone who wasn't of Japanese descent, young or old, contributed to the daily onslaught of gossip and rumors. Some shared what circulated among the many neighborhoods. There was a new attitude directed at the Nikkei. They were ignored. Their character was assassinated. They were accused of any wrongdoing and of carrying on clandestine affairs. They were looked down upon. It was as if all Nikkei carried incurable and infectious diseases. They were virtually shunned.

Tan Felomenia, a CHamoru woman (familian Pilåko'), said her issei brother-in-law, who worked at the Sumai Power Plant for years, was suspected of being a spy for the Japanese. It was rumored that he had provided information to the Japanese that prompted the invasion of the island, beginning with the bombing and air raid on Sumai. *Litiku* (Amyotrophic Lateral Sclerosis) and *boddek* (Parkinsonism-dementia) were two afflictions that affected many locals. A nisei brother and sister, both stricken with *boddek* were suspected and eventually accused of infecting other people in their village. Tun Isidro (familian Nikno) told me of an elderly man with *litiku* who was said to have infected nearby neighbors with his disease. The elderly man was thought to be of Japanese descent because of his slanted eyes and light complexion until a family member disclosed that he was actually a CHamoru-Filipino who had strong Chinese features as it was part of his bloodline. Tun Isidro admitted sheepishly that he too feared he would be affected because he was also the elderly man's neighbor.

Clandestine affairs linking perceived extra-marital relationships among issei and nisei were circulated. Before long, talk of incest, indecency and other perverted inclinations circulated with wild abandon. The Nikkei was blamed for many incidents, ranging from burglaries, which were rare in those days, to unexplained damage to property, which was also rare, to stealing of clothes on clotheslines, or the picking of fruit off another person's property. Before long, total exclusion of the Nikkei was exercised in social, religious, and day-to-day relationships. Tan Frubidensia, a Chamoru-Filipina woman who chose to be sympathetic to the Nikkei, said it was heartbreaking. However, she, too, was soon subjected to rumors directed at her when it was disclosed that her sympathies to the perceived "enemies," shouldn't be ignored.

During the Japanese occupation, Japanese invaders forcefully took food and livestock from both CHamoru and Nikkei families. There was starvation during the occupation. Above all, attractive girls and many women experienced indignities, and a small number were subjected to being comfort women.

Boys, young men, uncles, and fathers were forced to build roads, bridges, forts, dugouts, pillboxes, and other physical tasks that usually began at sunup and ended at sundown. They usually were deprived of water or food.

Then there was the assignment of Nikkei families to the villages on the island. Tun Takayoshi "Jose" Okamitsu recalled that he was at the Tutuhan stockade when a military commander conducted a roll call of confined Nikkei families and announced each was assigned a village in which to move. They would build homes and establish official residences there. They weren't allowed to return to their previous homesteads in the villages, notably Hagåtña, which were their pre-war domiciles. He remembered how shocked many of the heads of families felt. When one questioned the commander about why they were being assigned and lumped together in groups of five, he responded that it was for their safety, and that it was for the best. No further questions were entertained.

Many Nikkei also changed their surnames because no one wanted to hire them with their Japanese surnames. They also removed anything Japanese from their physical being and in their households. They were ridiculed, mocked, abandoned and treated as near-slaves, not to mention that during the war, many more were made to witness beheadings, torture, and the massacre of countless men, women, and children, although some also lost their lives in similar manners.

Some of the interviewees did have fond memories, but almost all of them were moved to tears when talking about specific mistreatment when they were forced to witness blood-chilling episodes.

Once, in the young life of Tun Bonifacio M. Suchida, he and his family stood in a circle of onlookers as a group of men, women, and children were interrogated, then slapped, including a baby in the arms of his mother. Then the group was beheaded, and, as they fell into the huge gaping hole that was dug for them by Nikkei teenagers, laughter ensued from the soldiers and interpreters who were there. Tun Bonifacio and his family were forced to watch in horror and grief. Once the victims fell dead into the hole, the onlookers, most of whom were issei families, were told to applaud amid terror in their eyes and swallowed sobs. Tun Bonifacio never forgot that scene. Adding further insult, able-bodied nisei were instructed to bury the victims, sometimes with bare hands.

Tan Engracia Morita shared how her young brother led two goats into pasture at their ranchland in Aspenggao, Barigåda. He was accosted by a group of Japanese soldiers who told him to give up his charges and also demanded he tell them where his family's produce was hidden. He didn't adequately respond because he didn't know the mixture of Japanese and broken English that the soldiers were using, two languages he did not speak. They whipped him mercilessly with the rope that he had tied the goats with. His punishment was so severe that the boy crawled to the family home where he died days later. The family sought help. No one came despite attempts at summoning a *suruhåna* and a CHamoru nurse from a village several miles away.

At the close of the war, not one Nikkei person that I interviewed could relate to being included in the long perilous trek to Manenggon. One *åmko'* (elderly) suggested perhaps Nikkei children (possibly young sansei), who were with CHamoru grandparents or neighbors, might have marched to Manenggon, but most Nikkei patriarchs and matriarchs had already committed self-exile when it was apparent that they weren't accepted into CHamoru households. They weren't trusted and were considered traitors. All spoke of being pillaged of goods, provisions, and livestock in their areas of confinement.

All spoke of being confined to the stockade in Tutuhan or Hågat and being subjected to inoculations; the taking of unexplained daily specimens of urine, feces and blood; and of being assigned to villages, where they would now live, nearly five years after the war.

All Nikkei families lost their original properties from before the war, including land that was never returned to them. Records are sketchy and, likely because of the American bombardment and the destruction of terrain and vegetation, nothing was ever substantiated about compensation of personal property from homes and villages, especially in Hagåtña where many businesses were owned by issei merchants. None of the interviewees were able to tell me what happened to possessions, houses, businesses, and merchandise. They noted that no one from the naval government or municipal leaders explained the outcomes of a pursuit regarding the return of or compensation for real property and other possessions. A prosperous issei merchant, who owned vehicles that he used for his pre-war business deliveries, claimed that the Japanese officials used them when they occupied his house in Hagåtña. His vehicles were used for local transportation but were doled out for use among other officers. At the close of the war, all the vehicles had been piled up, one on top of the other, and set on fire. A descendant of the businessman, Tan Magdalena Matsuyama, told me of this account.

The joy of being liberated for both CHamoru and Nikkei helped them overcome the anxiety and fear they experienced during the occupation. Many told me that relief from their suffering was what occupied their minds. From sheer gratitude, questions that nagged at many issei or nisei were left for later pursuits, but perhaps through rebuilding and resettling, were forgotten. They, like everyone else, were rebuilding their lives, staying quiet and unobtrusive, as it was best to just maintain dignity through a position of silence.

From my interviews, I learned about atrocities. I learned about kindness and kinship that the interviewees experienced during pre-war Guam. I learned about life in the capital city of Hagåtña, the fear that permeated throughout the Japanese occupation, and even indignities perpetrated by locals against Nikkei families while confined in the stockades at Tutuhan or Hågat. Appalling, too, was that after the war and into the '60s, while Guam was recovering, subdued or blatant cruelty against the Nikkei became common.

CHAPTER 6

The Stories Must Be Told

In the following chapters, I did my best with the information shared with me to tell the stories of Guam's Nikkei. I gave them voices — first-person voice to my grandfather, Zenpei Jito, my first cousin Jiro', and me. I gave third-person voices to the individuals who shared their stories, thoughts, sentiments, fears, worries, relief, and joy.

I interviewed my first cousin, Jiro' who gave much better accounts of my grandfather as he had known him. We connected our stories — what was shared with me by my mother and older relatives who grew up before the war. Although accounts of the other nisei and sansei don't appear as actual dialogue, their information is embedded in the story, befitting their recollections.

The information I share is gleaned from the "talk story" format. It is how I share my upbringing, which I recollect with vividness and accuracy. And how others shared their memories of those early days of the 20th century, pre-war, and the dark days of the occupation.

"Talk story" is storytelling. I picked up this new term at the countless Festivals of Pacific Arts (FESTPAC) that I've been to in the Cook Islands, the Samoas, Palau, the Solomons, and Guam when the island hosted the 12th FES-TPAC in 2016. In all these festivals, I participated as a storyteller, and learned this moniker as most of the delegations from Oceania used it in their art form. I embraced it as it made sense to me. As in all things with culture, people use storytelling to perpetuate the mindset of a community rich in folklore, beliefs, values, and attitudes.

Therefore, I firmly hold in my heart that their stories must indeed be told. I hope that the succeeding generations of many of these families, some still on Guam, others who no longer live on the island, and perhaps others who have moved on into the afterlife but have offspring scattered on this vast earth, will know that the original inhabitants who came from the land of the rising sun, did contribute, survive and withstand the tyranny of a time that wasn't of their choosing. Their stories are immense, thought-provoking, and, to me, sometimes difficult to digest.

They were genuine and sincere. There was no reason to be fictitious or to lie about ordeals. They talked freely without fear, for as Tun Florencio Yoshida said, "Esta måkpo' i gera, ya sa' håfa na bai hu fandagi put ayu ni' hu fakcha'i gi ayu na tiempo, debidi u måhgong todu i achåki sa' si Yu'os mås tumungo'." He expressed that the war was over so why would he lie about what he faced then; healing from that unfortunate time must happen because only God knew what transpired.

Also, they didn't know me aside from the fact that I was Nan Li'a' CHetton's grandson, Auntie Måme's son, Jiro's cousin, or that I was of the Balitres, CHetton, and Galaide' family clan.

Here are their stories.

PART TWO

CHAPTER 7

Goamu and Tokcha'
ZENPEI

I'm Zenpei Jito Onodera. I am originally from Oyama City of Tochigi-ken, which is 75 kilometers from Tokyo. My father's name was Hanzaburo Onodera from the same city. My biological mother died when I was very young. My father then married Saku Mori, who was from Ibaraki. She raised me along with the children she had with my father. I had four sisters: Kura (later Homoriya, married name) was born after me; then Hama (later Nakajima, married name); Yasu (later Kimura, married name); and the last one was Kimi (later Seki, married name). My only brother was Katsuji (married to Take Terauchi) who was born before Kimi. In Japanese culture, there was no word or distinction, at least from my recollection, for half-brothers, half-sisters or step-siblings.

I remembered the bitter winter of my departure from the family home. I bade farewell to my father, mother, and siblings, and made the half-walk, half-ride to Yokohama to board the Dai Ichi Tora Maru owned by Shimizu-sama. He had spoken at our town's main hall seeking to hire men from my prefecture to work at a copra plantation in Goamu, an island somewhere in the Pacific Ocean. He talked about working on a tropical island.

I knew nothing about tropical weather and copra. There were no words for them that I could relate to. Even a plantation was described as something that wasn't a form of farming in Japan. The meanings were not clear to the dozens of young men who sat spellbound, in awe of a job thousands of miles away.

We asked Shimizu-sama to describe coconut trees because we could not conjure an image of them ourselves. He said the trees were tall with branches that reached into the sky, with brown fruits ready to be picked by steady and strong hands. He also said we didn't have to worry about winter clothing as it was sunny and rainy throughout the year. He did mention *taifun*, which was a heavy storm that could last up to a little more than 24 hours.

He said there were no earthquakes and no tsunamis, and many of our parents gasped in relief, so loud that you could hear them throughout the huge room where Shimizu-sama spoke. Being that he was Japanese and spoke the language quite well, our parents trusted him especially when he said he lived on the island of Saipan and Goamu. He had a family in both places. He also spoke the native language.

He said he lived in the islands for as long as he had lived in Japan. He was, as he described himself, an issei. That was the first time I heard the word pronounced in such a fashion, almost a shock to many of the elders as well, although it was said with humility.

With the few clothes that we packed and the food provisions that were supposed to last the two weeks of anticipated travel, we didn't need anything else except a form signed by ourselves and our parents. The form explained that we would be working at this plantation for one year with the option of continuing for another year and every year after that.

Shimizu-sama explained that Goamu officials only granted him workers from Japan for a year at a time. He assured our parents that he'd pay us every two weeks, provide a place to stay, three meals a day, and whatever other needs we might have. He also told them that he'd bring us back to Yokohama, and it'd be up to us to find transport back to our homes. He was, to many of us would-be workers, very sincere and honest, answering every question that was asked.

I didn't know until I was in Goamu that many of us who had found our way to Yokohama harbor were joined by others from Gunma and Ibaraki. Our prefectures were neighbors. It was a relief that we would be working together because, although I didn't know many of the other young men from my own prefecture, we could comfortably socialize and become friends. Some of the surnames bound for Goamu were Hamamoto, Iwatsu, Miyasaki, Okada, Sakamoto, Sugiyama, and Yamanaka.

On top of all that, we were all young — teenagers for the most part. Save for a few who were perhaps 20 years old or so. I was only 15 years old, and there were many of us close to the same age. I remembered that there were two or three young men who were just 13 or 14 years old. We numbered about 30 passengers headed to Goamu. Saipan was another destination the ship would head to after Goamu.

We disembarked at the port of entry that was called Åpla' or, as I learned later, Apra Harbor. Along with the other newly hired copra plantation workers, Shimizu-sama had us stand in a straight line while we were each scrutinized by a guard.

Shimizu-sama announced each of us by name when he handed over the contract paper. We had to sign our names again. The guard frowned when each of us wrote the Japanese *kanji* (Japanese form of writing) on the form. Shimizu-sama explained in CHamoru that we did not speak English and followed orders based on his direction, and only in the Japanese language. He was known to port officials because he and his ships made periodic entries into Guam. They thought him to be reliable, honest, and trustworthy. The guard nodded and gave us his okay, shown with a stamp of approval on our forms. Shimizu-sama, I later learned, was also a rich man.

Another guard made a hasty study of our bodies, sizing us up from head to toe — a quick examination of our heads for indications of lice and inside our mouths for a quick look for some abnormality. Not sensing any form of physical deformity, we were perhaps declared physically fit. We appeared healthy without a cough or fever, and with muscles protruding from our skinny bodies; he nodded in satisfaction and bade us to go on our way. We boarded a bus, the only one of its kind on that lonely stretch of pavement. We were soon on our way to what we were told was a place called Tokcha'.

On our bus ride, we quietly took in the bumpy road and the unfamiliar vegetation that lined the road. There were no maple trees; no *fuji* (wisteria), *sakura* (cherry blossoms), plum, or strawberries; no familiar looking orchards of other fruits; and no gardens of daffodils and chrysanthemums. Everything was new and indeed, foreign to us.

We saw a few people walking on the side of the road. Some carried what looked like weeds under their arms. Some carried woven baskets filled with clothes, fruits, or something dark and covered in soil. There were no oxen or cows. There were none of the familiar orange-clad Buddhist monks who walked in the streets of our towns as they begged for their living.

Trees were everywhere and there was foliage that seemed to produce fruits and maybe vegetables. The many houses we passed were thatched, some with rusty tin sides. These types of homes did not exist even in the most destitute of our towns. Vegetation, however, appeared green and alive as compared to the ashen gray, almost white in winter-worn, snowless Tochigi when I had left.

We welcomed the blazing sunlight as the towns we left behind were in the harshest bitter, cold, gray of winter. It wasn't long before some of the passengers took off shirts to enjoy the heat of the day and the warmth of the sunny breeze that blew into the windows of our vehicle. The heat soon kicked up clouds of dust that seemed to follow us. In the back of their minds, everyone had visions of coconut trees and what to expect of them, as we would be working with them. Little did we realize that we were passing them in wild abandon, many in undisciplined rows, or scattered and uncultivated, but certainly at one with nature.

It took a while to arrive at our destination as our driver, Japanese too, but living in Guam for a while, told us the names of places and things that we saw. We saw an animal much like that of a cow, only bigger, darker, and with horns. It was later said, after much-repeated pronunciations, that it was a *karabao*. I didn't see horses, cows, much less, the oxen that I mentioned earlier. The driver said horses were not common in those days, but that cows usually were in the fields of private homeowners, and there weren't that many on the small island.

The bus made its way into a jungle canopied by huge trees. Everywhere, there were clearings filled with crude huts, which we were told were the center of the plantation.

This was Tokcha', our place of work and our home for the year. Shimizu-sama was the first to disembark as he went to his quarters to change into leisure clothes. Another gentleman, without speaking at all, led us to an open-sided, thatched-roof dwelling that was to be the lunchroom.

On a long table that was made from roughhewn slabs of coconut trees, or so we were told, and benches made of the same, we were instructed to sit and help ourselves to the noonday meal. The meal consisted of cooked rice, fried fish, fresh daikon, fried eggplant, and local onions, along with a sauce that I took an immediate liking to. They told us the sauce was *fina'denne'*, consisting of hot chili peppers, vinegar, and sea salt, along with green onions.

Instead of green tea, we were given pitchers of fresh local rainwater that came from a catchment alongside the roofing of this outdoor eating place. We welcomed the nutritious meal because we were hungry from the long ship ride. We were allowed seconds, and a few had third helpings.

While eating, Shimizu-sama spoke to us. He thanked us again and welcomed us to his plantation. He said that his other plantation was in northern Guam, called Hinapsan and that there were workers there, too. He said the men there also came from the same places we all came from and were recruited simultaneously, but their assigned plantation was different from ours. I wasn't sure whether the plantation at Hinapsan was bigger than the one in Tokcha' or vice-versa, but he said, from time to time, depending on the weather or circumstances, many of us, as well as many of them, would alternate places and positions in times of need.

He told us that Tokcha' as well as Hinapsan weren't restricted places. We could come and go as we wanted. He explained that Sundays were our days off. Shimizu-sama was Catholic, married to a CHarmoru wife. She insisted that Sunday, which was her sabbath, would be an appropriate day off for us to enjoy and be at ease as the work week was meant to be physically exhausting.

That part was true. We also had to go to Mass every Sunday.

We had a place to live and to sleep. It was to be our official home. Shimizu-sama expected that work hours be adhered to diligently, as copra production was as timely as orders were frequent and must be met for shipment from Goamu. If someone was sick and missed work, their time was covered by designated supervisors. If someone missed a day of work, their position still had to be filled to meet production quotas. Shimizu-sama didn't want to start setting restrictions of any sort but explained that he'd treat insubordination and disrespect accordingly. No one would know of such matters as his policy wasn't to divulge unnecessary information because that would cause disruption.

It appeared to the workers that Shimizu-sama was a fair man and was very considerate. Shimizu-sama's first meeting with us made us glad to have been given the opportunity to work. He explained one major restriction: The copra plantation was strictly off-limits to non-copra individuals because of dangerous equipment on the premises. Only the workers who operated the machines knew how to safely operate and maintain the equipment. Injuries to copra workers would be the only ones covered for medical treatment; therefore, visitors needed to be monitored all the time. The men nodded in agreement.

The men were bachelors. Shimizu-sama announced that once a contract ended and a young man wanted to return to his home in Japan, he'd be returned with a clean bill of health. This would involve a complete medical exam to make sure a sexual disease wasn't brought back to the country. In a humorous anecdote, Shimizu-sama said that any man wanting to have a mistress or wanting to engage in a clandestine affair might do so, provided it was conducted in private and with discretion. He said that with a knowing wink at all of us. He also suggested that in order to conduct a sexual liaison or activity, many times clearing his throat while discussing the subject, he urged that a blanket or two must completely cover our movements on our beds. Much later, the blankets were draped over the mosquito nets that all the workers acquired from our home country. With grins, chuckles, and even laughter he advised that sounds of nature must be kept to a minimum or that they be subdued or stifled. His final note was that bedding must always be changed after a rendez-vous. Washing them was our personal responsibility.

True to his word, every two weeks, we received our pay. He taught us how to adjust from yen to the dollar and vice-versa. We took an immediate crash course in financial transactions and soon became familiar with exchange rates. Shimizu-sama contracted someone from the Western Union, who worked at the main local bank, to be at the plantation so that the men could send home part of their earnings to help their families. I sent home whatever I could as I saw no need to spend extravagantly. The company fed us and provided our clothes, bedding, and toiletries. Laundry needs such as soap, bleach, and clothes pins were also included.

There were no major forms of transportation, and walking long distances from place to place was discouraged unless in small groups. By then, stories of the boogeyman, locally known as *taotaomo'na*, began to circulate among the men, and no one wanted to offend the spirits of their new home. The men behaved and were mostly content to just stay at the plantation.

Shimizu-sama made life pleasant for us at the plantation. In gratitude, we made extra sure that we didn't waste anything. By the same token, none of us missed work for any reason. The less we saw of him, the better for everyone because that meant there weren't any complaints, or he was, perhaps, con-centrating on the business of copra as well as his store in downtown Hagåtña.

CHAPTER 8

Training at the Plantation
ZENPEI

The first several weeks at Tokcha' tested our mental abilities. Local men, whom I suspected were probably near our age, first taught us that the coconut tree was the tree of a thousand uses. The first lesson was recognizing and memorizing the names of the various parts of the tree.

Because we only spoke Japanese, we had to learn the CHamoru words right away for each part of the coconut. The local boys who taught us had never been to Japan or any of the prefectures, and they certainly didn't speak our language. We didn't have these trees back home, so everything was taught in the CHamoru language. We had to identify and know the tree parts at a glance: *fåha', gunot, åpplok, baina, ha'ef, pengka, bobolong, patnitos, hagåssas, må'son, daddek, hågon, niyok*, and a whole lot more.

In addition, there were by-products from the tree. The first product we learned about was *tuba*. Tuba came as a sap sliced a quarter of an inch daily from the *pengka*. The sap was caught through a sieve from the tree called the *gunot*. As the sap oozed into a container, the day's sap, from the fresh cut, was then emptied into a gallon that stored the sweet sap. Once a gallon became full, it was then drunk with relish, either as a soothing beverage or on a festive occasion, it functioned as an alcoholic beverage. Its alcoholic properties also served as a laxative. Tuba could be produced as a syrup for pancakes, fried bananas, or yam doughnuts. When the tuba fermented, it became vinegar after being left alone for a few days.

There was *bukåyu*, which involved grated coconut. When pan-fried with huge amounts of sugar, the sugar slowly melted, thickened, then hardened with the coconut. Once cooled, it became candy. On that first day of indoctrination, we had our first taste of it. It was a favored dessert at parties, as well as a leisurely snack.

When mixed with water, the grated coconut became milk that, when squeezed into a bowl, was suitable for soups and sauces. This gave any dish a delicious taste, especially when salt or sugar was added. The left-over grated coconut was then given to fowl and pigs as feed.

There was *låña*, which was oil used in cooking as well as an ointment for the body. Producing the oil took days of cooking over an open fire. The coconut milk, in huge pots, was boiled for a long period until it produced the desired look and feel of oil. Several adults are needed to make the oil as the cooking could not be interrupted, and the fire needed the constant addition of firewood. The layers of oil and fat that accumulated at the boiling point had to constantly be stirred and sifted, and additional coconut milk had to be added. The boiling was watched carefully so that the final oil had the desired properties. Oil from the coconut was ideal for frying fish, chicken, pork, beef, and stir-fried vegetables. It also was used as an ointment for aching joints and muscles. When heated on a large metal spoon over a burning candle, the hot oil was spread as an ointment over abdomens, soothing stomach aches.

A separate work crew was established to produce the oil. When cooled, it was left to sit for a few days. The oil was constantly spilled through a wire screen mesh to remove remnants and other debris. The oil was then poured into gallons, bottles, and vials that were sold at the Shimizu store. Customers bought it as cooking or frying oil, salves, and ointments.

Women, too, were hired on the plantation, but they were local and didn't stay at the plantation. Shimizu-sama's wife supervised them, and they served under her employ. Their employment wasn't included in the payroll manifests of the copra workers. They had duty usually from 9 a.m. to 5 p.m. daily except Sundays, and had separate entrances, exits, bathrooms, and a work site that was mainly a kitchen. They made trays of *bukåyu* daily. The candy became favored orders from families who wanted it as dessert at many *fi'esta* gatherings, parties, and religious observances.

In addition, many of the women baked bread and other sweet pastries. All the work crews loved and looked forward to a thinly sliced local cake spread over a large flat tray with a custard-like concoction spread over it. A sprinkle of cinnamon gave this dessert an extra appeal. The dessert was called *latiya*, which, because of the lack of the letter "L," in our language, we gingerly called it *ratiya*. Every Friday before the ladies knocked off from work, our evening meal included the delicious *ratiya*. The trays were always wiped clean. We loved and looked forward to the dish.

The green coconut's fruit was called *månha*, which has a soft flesh. The soft meat could be eaten raw, or it could be set to dry and then further ground, producing a flour that was ideal for tortillas. The *månha's* soft meat, too, could be made into pies with meringue as its topping. The tortillas and pies were made by the women who made the *bukåyu* and *ratiya*, but the tortillas were usually done at the request of Mrs. Shimizu as she'd give them to families as a form of social *chenchule'* (gift giving). They weren't sold at all.

When a coconut turned brown, it was then husked. At this stage, the meat had naturally hardened. From the brown coconut came the copra, which was the purpose of the plantation's operation. Both green and brown coconuts contained potable and sweet liquid, which quenched people's thirst.

Palm fronds were woven into hats, fans, baskets of all sizes, and thatch for the roofing of dwellings. A few of the men learned how to weave just by watching many of the adept workers. This knowledge became useful when thatch was needed to replace worn-out roofing at some of our shelters.

The lumber from the tree was used to construct buildings and furniture, much like the lunch tables and benches at our mess hall.

Other parts of the tree were used as adornment, decorations, and toys, one of which I learned to make and use, a whistle that actually worked. There were others to learn. It was fascinating.

The coconut was indeed the producer of a thousand wonders, and the many things that came from it were extremely useful, practical, and limitless. Every day consisted of a visual and word connection that we had to master.

The coconut, from seedlings, saplings, fruits, limbs, fronds, and trees provided housing, clothing, utensils, nourishment, utilitarian uses, decorations, ropes, alcohol and oil, lumber, livestock feed, medication, weapons, and everything that one's mind could conjure.

Not only did the coconut tree and its various parts provide all these necessities, but the processed meat for copra, while laborious to prepare, provided a necessary long-term income that funded imports of needed goods, other merchandise, and even fruits, vegetables, canned goods, vehicles, appliances, machinery of sorts, furnishings, fashions, hardware, and other necessities to the island.

There was also the physical aspect of conquering the coconut tree. This required exertion, stamina, and balance. We learned how to plant, cultivate, and watch the trees grow from one stage to the next, where a by-product resulted. We learned patience, knowledge, and science. It took years to fully know the coconut and its many wonders.

We had to master climbing up and down the long stretch of the tree, barefoot and with our arms hugging the long tree limbs until we reached the top, where the nuts were nestled in the branches. When the trees were mature and strong, we scaled them in seconds, and from atop, we perched and balanced ourselves on a sturdy frond. We'd then wrestle the brown, ripe fruits, separating them from green bunches. We'd watch them crash to the ground. We had to make sure that they hit no one, especially on their heads. A falling coconut hitting someone on the head could knock the person unconscious.

The plantation overseers divided the men into different work groups that were part of an established system where each group was assigned to one specific task. It resembled an assembly line of copra production. Copra was called *sine'so'* in CHamoru. Everyone had to know all the work involved from planting to climbing, harvesting, husking, grating, and then processing. The assigned work was set as shifts to accommodate an ongoing, non-stop process. It took a long time to refine this method of work. Before long, the men were drawn into the routine that defined their livelihood.

We adjusted to life on the plantation. We kept our living quarters clean. We left no trash on the grounds. We disposed of trash by burning it every evening at dusk after we ate our dinner. No one could claim the sighting of a rat anywhere. We also burned coconut husks as we discovered that they made excellent mosquito chasers. Every Sunday, on our days off, we'd lay bedding, pillows, blankets, and our laundry atop bushes along the beach at Tokcha'. The more delicate fabrics like underwear, handkerchiefs, short *hapi* coats, and even socks were hung with clothes pins on lines made from coconut fiber that were fashioned into ropes.

We had to adjust to the mosquitoes and flies that settled on our food whenever we ate, which we constantly shooed away — a momentary break in this routine would have swarms of them descending on our plates. There were also termites. I never experienced termites in our town. The mosquitoes and flies in Oyama City arrived in huge swarms from late spring to just before autumn when the weather got colder. On the island, it was throughout the year, every day. After the first month of our stay, we wrote home for mosquito netting that was made in one of the towns. Our families sent them to us, and before long, we included the washing of the mosquito netting in our laundry.

CHAPTER 9

Learning Goamu

ZENPEI

We fished at Tokcha'. We caught *gåmson* (octopus). We harvested the green grapelike clusters of *addo'* (seaweed) and learned to pickle them. We caught *påhgang* (clam), *balåte'* (sea cucumbers that we'd cut up, clean out their insides, and leave to dry on woven coconut leaf mats), and *palos* (saltwater eels) that sometimes got trapped during low tide. We learned to cook with coconut milk. What was missing on Guam's beaches was the seaweed that produced the *nori* that wrapped *sushi*. That part of our Japanese cuisine, we missed tremendously.

By then, two issei, Yokoi and Guioko, discovered the Manenggon River. On Sundays we'd spend the day there after our mandatory attendance for Mass at the nearby church. We swam, barbecued, and fished. The locals, who were now our friends, joined us with their families and taught us more about trapping and shooting the wild pigs or deer that were plentiful in the jungle. Many had weapons that were chiefly used for hunting. Although they allowed us to use their guns, we were wary of shooting at fruit bats and birds high in the trees, so we left them alone, out of respect. We learned the word *picnic*, but it was an American word that the CHamoru used. It was a delightful pastime. Among us issei, the consumption of tuba was like our *sake*, and for our older CHamoru friends, it was just an intoxicant. Somewhere in our grasp of learning, we also learned the term *åguayente*. I'm not sure how that came about, but

I think it possibly involved the coconut sap in its fermented stage, but I'm not sure. It was an alcoholic beverage, much stronger than tuba.

In the river at Manenggon, we caught shrimp, eel, catfish, and freshwater fish called *tilåpia*, which was delicious when cooked in coconut milk or fried in coconut oil. Manenggon was a delight for us all.

From our local friends, we also learned the names of fish from the ocean behind our plantation, and the various ways of cooking them. There was *tataga'* (unicorn), *mafute'* (snapper), *sesyon* (rabbit), *tagåfi* (red snapper), *atuhong* (parrot), *gådao* (grouper), as well as the *mañåhak* (juvenile rabbit), *ti'ao* (goat-fish), and others.

With the fish and creatures of both the ocean and rivers, such as octopi and shrimp, we were taught to make *kelaguin, which we could spice with hot chili peppers and green onions. Then, we would soak the mixture in lemon juice or tuba vinegar and sea salt*. The dish was delicious, but it was pika (spicy hot) when there were too many chili peppers. We learned that word very early on, and we muttered it constantly.

We learned CHamoru, the language. Our local friends corrected my use of the word, Goamu. It was the name of the island of Guam. I learned a few cusswords but soon enough, we were having short conversations in CHamoru, and that expanded to full conversations without the cuss words.

Before long, the rest of us issei conversed in CHamoru and just ignored Japanese. It was a comfortable adjustment. We never spoke English and had no reason to as many of the CHamoru didn't speak it at all. The only other language that was spoken was Spanish as, we were told, it was the language of the Catholic church.

I wasn't sure how true that was. Many of us on the plantation started going to village churches. We didn't pay much attention to the religious ritu-als for the hour-long service, as we just followed what everyone was doing. It involved a lot of kneeling, which we were told was *dimu* in CHamoru, standing, and sitting when necessary. We also did the sign of the cross constantly. We'd watch people walk single file toward the priest, who would then put a white wafer in their mouths. We were taught the word *ostia* or the Holy Eucharist, but we weren't allowed to take it unless we were baptized. We had no idea what that meant, as the word "baptize" held no meaning for us. My favorite part, I'd admit, was the beautiful songs sung by the church faithful. Because they were repetitious at every Mass, we were soon humming the tunes. Some of us managed to sing a few verses. We also sang the songs while we were working. It was soothing and helped ease fatigue on a lot of days.

Every year contracts ended. Many of us renewed to stay for another year. Some decided to return home. Shimizu-sama accompanied them on return voyages and recruited replacements in the same towns. He would always come by the plantation around the early part of February. He'd bring not just the replacement workers, but also mail and gifts from our families — fruits in season such as strawberries, plums, pecans, pears, and apple pears, decorations, and home knickknacks that he'd pass out to the workers. He made sure there was something for everyone no matter how small the item was. The most favored item that he brought was the *yukata*, which was the dress down *bahåkke* (leisure house or yard attire). The *yukata* was quite similar in meaning. We'd wear these clothes around our quarters as bathrobes and as pajamas, or going to and from the toilets that were referred to as outhouses. The CHamoru word was *kommon sanhiyong*.

On one notable return trip, Shimizu-sama brought the plantation workers a pair each of *geta*, wooden clogs. The clogs were ideal because the rainy season submerged the grounds in nearly an inch of muddy water and made walking outside messy for us. The *geta*, when worn, towered a few inches off the ground, which saved us from washing our feet when entering our sleeping quarters. We all found relief with our footwear. The grounds didn't have concrete or wooden floors so you couldn't hear the tell-tale clip-clop sounds that the clogs made while we walked.

Another nice experience was the Christmas and New Year celebrations. We originally weren't familiar with the holidays, but at the urging of Shimizu-sama's wife, they'd bring us to a *misan gåyu*, which was the midnight Mass. When translated it meant Mass for a rooster. We didn't understand as we never saw a rooster at a Catholic church, but we'd hear the crowing of several at a time once the clock struck midnight.

Afterward, we gathered at Shimizu-sama's home in Hagåtña for refreshments of fried yam doughnuts that were called *buñelos dågu*. They were tasteless but perked up when dipped in syrup that was made from the coconut sap. We drank coffee and something called cocoa, but never green tea. We had gotten used to green tea's absence from our daily consumption. Then, there were Christmas bonuses of $20 that Shimizu-sama gave to us in envelopes with Christmas cards. The $20 excited us. Christmas day was a holiday, and so was New Year's day. So, we had two special days off a year, in addition to the Sundays that were very much regular and strictly followed with devotion.

CHAPTER 10

I am Issei
ZENPEI

Life was pleasant and uneventful. While we knew our life on the plantation was pretty much routine, training new recruits was the only major disruption. It would take time for many of the new workers to learn the words and descriptions of the coconut tree, the growth stages, the skill of coconut tree climbing, as well as the other tasks of husking, grating, cutting the meat from their shells, and filling gunny sacks that were to be shipped to foreign ports.

A big challenge was the learning and memorization of the CHamoru words for the various parts of the tree. At dusk, some of us took new recruits, and we'd walk around the grounds pointing things out and having them repeat the words that we now knew by heart. There was lots of laughter. Some confused the words as they were also being taught vulgar words. A few mixed them up quite often. It took time, but once that was mastered, life on the plantation focused on other adjustments.

Sundays became a serious, most sought-after day. As soon as darkness hit the plantation on Saturday night, many would begin the long walk to parts of the island, often in groups of three to five. Some would be seen hustling off to Hagåtña, which was the center of nightlife and speakeasies. By then, many of us spoke comfortable CHamoru and were not harassed or bothered by anyone.

Many of the men brought along extra clothes, neatly folded, and gingerly placed in gunny sacks. They would change in the boondocks to catch a parish Mass at the break of dawn. Footwear wasn't a problem, but the *geta* was a definite no-no because of the clacking sound it made on wooden floors and pavement. Extra shoes were also brought in case it was raining, but they made sure they didn't step into muddy pools or animal feces. Instead, they cautiously walked on the grassy side of paths, trails, and roads. Many of the men were in search of a good-looking CHamoru girl to court. Romance was in their hearts and I, too, was caught up in it.

It was at church that we'd often see beautiful CHamoru girls. Many of us were always tongue-tied and couldn't muster the memorized greeting of "Håfa Adai." *Buenas* was easier, and it seemed appropriate to use it in church as that was where I'd hear it muttered constantly, followed by a sentence or two in Spanish. We plantation workers stuck together and were too bashful to attempt courtship of any sort.

By then, I began sending less money home to Oyama City, and I began saving whatever I could, thanks to the continued visits of people from the Western Union. Included among them was also a teller who took cash deposits from us and gave us bank books that were updated with individual deposits every pay period. Many of us began feeling more secure. By then, I decided that Guam was now my legal home. I'd made my final decision to spend the rest of my life on the island.

Before I made that decision, I wondered about my family in Japan. I knew that the earnings I sent home helped them tremendously, as the letters that I'd get would tell me how the money was spent. At first, my mother would list items that were purchased. In a return letter, I told her that the money they received from me was to be spent on whatever they could get and no listing was necessary. I'd also get letters about seasonal sicknesses like the flu. My father was now having difficulties with gout and muscle spasms. Of course, I prayed for them. As I told them about life on the island, they were fascinated that we were right next to the ocean and that fish and seafood were plenty. Tochigi is landlocked. It would take several days of trekking by vehicle and by foot before an ocean could be reached; and if reached, the water in that part of the country was bitter cold, so fishing was done in boats and other vessels.

It wasn't ideal for swimming. Sunbathing didn't come to mind because it was always cold even in the summer.

I realized one day that I was an issei. I was enjoying my young adulthood and thoughts of having a wife and children began to percolate in my mind.

My companions in the plantation began sharing similar thoughts. We soon began discussing the young ladies we'd see at church and noticing their appearance, dress, and their scents of coconut oil and lemon. My colleagues and I would talk about them a lot. Our discussions never centered on kimono-clad damsels. Our words about romance were absent of anything Japanese. We were slowly incorporating the use of CHamoru even amongst ourselves.

Often, I'd spend the day in Hagåtña. By then, issei businessmen had made their mark in the commercial district. They included our own JK Shimizu, J. Haniu, F. Suzuki, M. Hirano, T. Ooka, T. Shinohara, G. Kurokawa, A. M. Fujikawa, H. S. Sakakibara, and a Sawada. There also were two businesswomen — a Mrs. A. Hirano and Mrs. T. Dejima. For a Japanese or foreign businessman to be licensed, he must be married to a local CHamoru. It was the law. I wasn't sure if the two women were married to CHamoru men. If they were, I didn't know who they were. When I later took over the management of the plantation, I realized why Mrs. Shimizu-sama played an important role in the business of the plantation. She was CHamoru, plus, through Tåtan Kåcha's license, their marriage allowed him to hire us and bring us over from Japan.

When I left the plantation much later and started a business in Hagåtña, I received my business license because of my wife.

An advertisement in the *Guam Recorder* showed a JOTA Bottling Works. It showed all kinds of sparkling water, but the owner's name wasn't listed in the ad, only the company. It could have possibly been an issei owner with Jota as a surname. Jota, to me, was a Japanese surname. But I wasn't sure.

And then one day, I saw her. I, along with my friends Sudo, Asanoma, Yamashita, and Murakami were at the annual Sånta Marian Kåmalin Mass at the Hagåtña Church. Her name was Maria, and her friends called her Li'a'. She was pretty and petite. It was she who gestured to me, asking if the pew I was in was available for her and her friends to sit. I nodded yes. I couldn't keep my eyes off her. Before Mass that morning, my friends decided to each take a separate pew so the young ladies would ask for available seats next to them. I was the first to achieve this success, and it wasn't long before my companions also had pewmates.

Sudo and Asanoma conversed with a bunch of girls, while Yamashita and Murakami appeared obviously nervous and alone at first, but because the capital city's church was the center of all Catholic activities, it was always packed. Glancing around the church, I noticed Haniu, Fujikawa, Akiyama, and Yoshida on the other side of the building. We were all enamored by the sight and scent of these veiled ladies in white, butterfly sleeves and floor-length dresses that covered their feet. All of them had waist-length, shiny black hair that smelled like lemon, and the entire church oozed with such a romantic scent. It was nice.

From that Mass, Maria and I became much better acquainted and a friendship ensued. Often, we'd go shopping, stopping in the many stores along the commercial side in Hagåtña. The commercial side was where businesses were situated, while behind them were the barrios where the resident families had their homes.

One day, Li'a', her sister, brother and I sat eating at the Jagatna Gas Kitchen that was owned by T. Shinohara. Other issei with their local girls accompanied by siblings or cousins also occupied various areas of the huge restaurant. Because the girls had strict mothers and fathers, siblings and cousins had to accompany them to the capital. Once, we were laughing at Suzuki because his girlfriend was accompanied by a maiden aunt, her grandmother, and her godmother. The three elders ordered the most expensive items on the menu, and Suzuki ended up paying with his recent paycheck.

It wasn't long before I and many others were soon joined by elderly folks, too. It was the most embarrassing moment of our lives. The siblings and cousins that were previously with us were relegated to house, ranch, and yard chores, while the replacement elderly chaperones soon enjoyed expensive meals in their stead. It drained our pockets. One night at bedtime, Suzuki was doubling over with laughter in our sleeping quarters because his initial predicament had now plagued the rest of us. Despite that bit of social angst, I still remembered how tasty those thick hamburgers were with the ice-cold Coca-Cola. Still, we all had a wonderful time at the Jagatna Gas Kitchen.

It wasn't long before I proposed and married Maria Cruz Bae Santos from Tomhom. Her parents were Juan Cruz Santos and Leonora de Bae of Sumai. Li'a' was the third of six children. Her other siblings in succession consisted of Juliana who was unmarried, Jesusa, then her (Li'a'), followed by a brother named Ramon, then Joaquin, and the youngest was Mercedes who married twice, first to a man from the *familian* Piyu with the surname of Castro and the other was from *familian* Buyak with the surname of Agualo'.

It was my wife's father or my father-in-law, Tun Juan, whose first name I took when I was baptized a Catholic. When the priest asked what Christian name I chose, without thinking, I automatically blurted Juan as my first name. I learned and adjusted to the a.k.a.names, as it was part of the CHamoru culture. Li'a' was from the CHetton clan, but the family was part of the huge family called Balitres that had other sub-clans like Fånggo, and others that I don't remember. Also, my mother-in-law, Leonora, was the eldest in the Galaide' family branch, whose roots were from Sumai.

I devoted my life to learning everything there was about my wife and new family, the in-laws. Thus, my integration into finally being an official issei took hold.

CHAPTER 11

Copra Production
ZENPEI

I dug deep into the rigors of the copra industry. I was soon supervising subordinate workers in the different facets of copra production, from picking to husking, then grating, and separating the clean meat from dirty meat, which usually happened when the brown shell of the coconut was processed into the meat. The grated coconut has to be clean and kept fresh or else it would affect quality and wouldn't be suitable for shipment, much less purchase by merchants marketing them in their respective countries.

Years later, Shimizu-sama invested in machinery that grated coconuts, which made work easier. That process allowed us to process huge volumes of coconuts, which increased our production quotas for shipment.

The good thing about the coconut was that it didn't naturally rot in its shell. It simply went from one stage to another, from *daddek* (seedling) to *månha* (green) to *niyok* (brown), and when left untended, especially on the ground, it developed another fleshy meat inside that was called *fåha'*, which was edible. If left intact, it would sprout roots and begin to grow into another healthy tree. When left alone, even when husked, it didn't spoil and rot away like many other fruits.

On the plantation, there were three issei who were older than most of the men, perhaps in their 30s, and held supervisory positions at the plantation. Like the rest of the men, they were contract hires, but they held high-level positions of authority assigned by Shimizu-sama.

These issei were all married and had left their wives and children in Japan. Tun Shinichiro Okamitsu came with two sons, one of whom stayed for a short time at the plantation. He discovered he couldn't climb halfway up the tall coconut trees. He complained about mosquitoes, flies, and the humidity. His younger son, Takayoshi, didn't work at the plantation, but he came often as his father felt homesick, especially when the older one named Kiyoshi quit after two months. Kiyoshi had found employment in one of the issei businesses in Hagåtña and stayed away from the plantation for the rest of the year, avoiding Tokcha' forever. Kiyoshi grew to hate the island. Takayoshi took to hanging out with the workers and was often there for outside activities like fishing, hunting, and spending time in Manenggon or Hagåtña. Tun Shinichiro wanted to stay after his first-year contract expired, but Kiyoshi pleaded with him to return home. The other son, Takayoshi, stayed and worked elsewhere but not at the plantation.

Takayoshi and countless other issei, like me, never returned to Japan, and instead, we all chose Guam as our permanent home.

The other issei were Tun Kensuke Inoki and Tun Bulengngo' Yanada. Tun Kensuke was handsome and muscular. It was rumored that he was having an affair with a CHamoru woman whom he met at a speakeasy, although no one ever confirmed his exploits. Some years later, when Tun Kensuke had already left Guam, a little boy in the village of Mangilao was said to be his offspring. As a teenager, that boy exhibited Tun Kensuke's features.

Tun Bulengngo' was a nickname for Yanada-san who had a flat nose and was bow-legged. Many of the workers often wondered if he could breathe through his nostrils. I found out later that the word *Bulengngo'* meant flat, I guess in reference to his nostrils. To not insult the man outright, one worker got the translation from one of the CHamoru men who was training us. Many wondered what the CHamoru word was for bow-legged as this physical attribute was more pronounced than his nose. It wasn't until much later that we learned the word, *patuleka*. Apparently, the CHamoru had given him the nickname. I never learned his real Japanese first name.

Tun Shinichiro worked the first year of the contract and returned home with Kiyoshi. Tun Kensuke and Tun Bulengongo' lasted three and four years respectively. I never found out if the latter two ever came back to Guam in later years. Tun Shinichiro was the foreman of the buildings and grounds. Tun Kensuke was the foreman of the machinery and equipment, and Tun Bulengngo' was the foreman of the shipment, cargo, and transport of the copra. After Tun Shinichiro's departure, Tun Bulengngo' took over the buildings and grounds in addition to his responsibilities. I didn't know if all three could speak fluent CHamoru. With the exception of those solely connected to plantation work, Japanese language was what kept them in sync among themselves. Learning English was not a priority for them.

I was eventually rewarded with several promotions in succession. I became supervisor of one major task after another until I was supervising all levels of the copra processing. I soon became a foreman of the plantation. It was then that I made my first venture to Hinapsan.

Prior to my going there, Tåtan Kåcha briefed me on my mission. Property owners were going to decide soon about whether they would continue to lease the property to Tåtan Kåcha. By then, from the locals, I learned that Shimizu-sama was well-respected in the community. He was socially crowned as the Mariana Islands Coconut King, a title that was made known by the locals that touted his successful copra plantation on the island. It didn't take long for all the workers to address him as Tåtan Kåcha. By the time war approached, myself, nisei, and some young sansei called him by his nickname and a.k.a. name. I no longer referred to him as Shimizu-sama. I grew accustomed to addressing him only as Tåtan Kåcha.

At Hinapsan, I made personal observations through inspection. The plantation was not as big as Tokcha'. It was perhaps 2 to 3 acres less in area and not as expansive as Tokcha', but it had more coconut trees based on my calculations. However, I also learned that the Hinapsan plantation did not have many workers, as the copra that was sent from there only went to the Philippines, India, Australia, and Indonesia.

The Philippines had started to establish its own copra plantations. They soon began to undermine the efforts of Tåtan Kåcha. *Taifuns* frequented the Philippines archipelago, and each time it hit their coastal and inland areas, the Marianas Maru was still in their ocean. The inclement weather rendered the copra from Guam useless as the shipment would get caught in the deluge of rain and ocean water that swept on board. Spoiled copra would be pushed into the sea by the crewmen. Those huge losses became unbearable. Later shipments would be diverted to Australia when requests from India and Indonesia lessened. From the Philippines, it stopped completely.

Tåtan Kåcha needed to quickly decide what to do as the most recent foreman of the Hinapsan plantation decided not to renew his contract because he started getting sickly. In his condition, trying to manage the plantation contributed to his lack of consistency and difficulty filling copra quotas for shipment. Tåtan Kåcha assigned one of his older sons to the job. His son wasn't performing well because he had come into the copra business late in the game. I was then tasked to take over the plantation's management. As it was a promotion, I was also handed the management of Tokcha' where the copra was shipped to Japan, Taiwan, San Francisco, Chile in the Southern Americas, and Panama.

It wasn't long before I began spending more time in Hagåtña as Tåtan Kåcha taught me the ways of shipping, dollar values, currency exchanges, shipping manifests and contracts with shipping magnates, and the foreign taxes imposed by the countries where copra was shipped. Each foreign government had strict guidelines that needed to be followed and shipping dates that included the shipment's arrival, quality, grade of the copra, and maritime laws that needed to be studied and learned.

I only went to Tokcha' and Hinapsan to hand out paychecks, and to see about the welfare of the workers as they were still sheltered, fed, and given provisions of toiletries and other supplies. The work was exhausting. I found myself falling asleep at the dinner table at home. My wife and children were caught off guard by my increased workload. The Sunday day off was my respite as it allowed me to sleep all day and into the night. Often on Sundays, Tåtan Kåcha also demanded that we meet. My wife often lied to him about tasks that

I was doing just to allow me much-needed rest.

When the Hinapsan property owners finally made the decision not to renew the lease for the property, a devastating *taifun* hit the island. This happened in the late '20s. At that time, Australia was the only country that maintained its shipment of copra contracts that year. Tåtan Kåcha had sent home workers whose contracts he didn't renew. He had me close the plantation, transfer equipment and tools to Tokcha', destroy buildings, secure salvageable belongings, do all the paperwork necessary for the business to cease, and conduct the bulldozing of the entire premises save for the coconut trees, many of which were destroyed by the *taifun*. My final act was to transact payments to vendors and creditors.

The *taifun* was a blessing, I thought, as the plantation already had lost income and production had decreased. The coconut trees would have been rendered useless for three to five years. Locals reported the storm was one of the worst to hit the island. The northern part of Guam was hit the hardest. I knew Tåtan Kåcha was hurt by Hinapsan's closure when I saw him crying when he thought he was alone. A handful of workers followed me to Tokcha'. From that group, there were Asano, Ichihara, Ige, Murafumi, Sakamoto, Takano, Tsuda, and Yamashiro.

When Hinapsan became no more, Tokcha' picked up the slack by incorporating Australia in its production quota. I returned to work there. It wasn't long before Tåtan Kåcha had me manage the entire plantation. It was soon after taking over the new responsibilities that Tåtan Kåcha had the bright idea to send me alone to do the recruitment in Gunma, Ibaraki, and Tochigi. I dreaded the sea voyage because of seasickness, but I also dreaded public speaking as I became flustered and tongue-tied. I could speak in front of the plantation workers, as it was conducted informally, often as mere casual conversation, but not in front of a huge group of strangers, many of whom were parents of those to be recruited, and in Japan, too. This was when I gave Tåtan Kåcha perhaps my first and only objection to his request. I told him no. I felt that he could ask me to do whatever he wanted, and I'd jump at the chance, but not a sea voyage and certainly not public speaking.

However, Tåtan Kåcha never took my refusal personally, his trust and belief in me was a source of pride.

Among us issei, I, too, became close to the men on the plantation and their families, especially those whom I arrived with who had stayed on through the years. I inadvertently found myself and my wife, as godparents to several nisei. Our wives made sure of that, so, it was no wonder that the circle of people that Tåtan Kåcha cultivated were soon his constant companions, including myself. I often felt that I was his right hand. This became a system of survival for us when war broke out.

CHAPTER 12

My Family and Other Nikkei
ZENPEI

My marriage was good. We had five children who became part of the island's crop of nisei. The eldest, a girl named Carmen, was born on June 6, 1913. My second daughter, Maria, was born on November 20, 1914. My third daughter, Ana, was born on July 14, 1916. My only son was Juan, whom everyone called John, born on February 3, 1918, and the youngest, a daughter, Agueda, was born on July 13, 1920.

I taught the Japanese language to all my children. All of them had a good grasp by the time they reached the age of six. However, they also knew CHamoru because both Li'a' and myself spoke CHamoru to them daily, despite my being told I was paya', a cross between stuttering and lisping, but my Japanese was smooth although rarely spoken. It was during the war when I had to caution the children not to speak Japanese ever, as myself and other issei refused to cooperate as translators with the invading forces. I insisted that the children always speak CHamoru, especially in the presence of relatives from their mother's side and especially among the Nikkei. Speaking Japanese during the occupation proved to be dangerous.

My first-born Carmen was dependable and adept at both fishing and hunting. She was the expert at catching and detecting octopus in crevices in the low tide near the reef. She provided octopus either as *kelaguin* or cooked in coconut milk with pumpkin tips, eggplants, and water spinach as our form of *chenchule'* at family functions. At night, she'd accompany a crowd of mostly boys to hunt coconut crabs, and, on nights of the full moon, the land crabs that were plentiful. She also husked and grated the coconuts that fed the crabs so that they'd be savory and free of internal parasites in time for cooking. Although she wasn't good at slingshots and other weapons, she was always the first to spot a colony of fruit bats high up in the trees. It was her brother Juan who caught them, and he was good at it. In addition, she helped Li'a' with housework and caring for her siblings, especially the youngest, Agueda.

Maria was meticulous and was our house girl who knew how to clean and organize. She could also cook up a storm and was the household's chef for all of our meals. By her mid-teens, we sent her out to be a housekeeper for many affluent CHamoru families. During the war, when it was learned by Japanese officials that she was a nisei, they took her as a housekeeper at many of the officer's quarters, often without compensation, but she was plied with foodstuffs like rice and daikon. Maria, whom we lovingly called Maikita was sort of a right hand to me. She'd be the one to accompany me to many of the issei homes that were employed by Tåtan Kåcha. Because she was my constant companion, I grew to rely on her for many tasks, which included sending her to deliver messages and carry goods that she could manage.

She was the first to give me a grandchild when she was not yet 16. In those days, it wasn't uncommon for young girls to have children early. It was accepted although such disclosure was kept isolated. She never told me who had fathered my first grandson, whom I began calling Jiro', which in Japanese referred to "the second son." Li'a' and I took him under our wing as he was precocious, energetic, and a talker. He wasn't yet six months of age when he began walking.

As he passed his toddler years and reached childhood, he became good at menial tasks and chores. I often took him with me to the plantation. He'd be by my side as I'd met with the copra workers. He was well-liked by the men. Like his mother, Jiro' was organized, meticulous, and respectful. I referred to him as a nisei. He was unlike his Uncle John, the older nisei. I felt that Jiro' was more of a son than a grandson.

Ana was often teamed with Maria for the housework and wasn't keen on outside tasks. However, by the time she was a teen, Li'a's unmarried sister, Nan Lånå' or Juliana, took her to rear as she had no children of her own. We only saw Ana at intervals such as holidays and other auspicious occasions like family celebrations. She lived with Nan Lånå' into her adult years, and, even when she married Felix Mesa, her aunt became a part of her household. Initially, Juliana lived in her own Quonset hut far up the hills in Tomhom where the CHetton clan resided.

Juan, my only son, was often up to mischief. He was good at hunting and fishing and often paired off with Carmen on many of the seasonal harvests. He'd only do as much as he wanted, never striving to go beyond his capabilities. He was also privy to lying. His sisters would accuse him of rummaging through their personal belongings looking for money. As a handsome young man, I could also tell that he was a womanizer as he was never without a female or two, sometimes three, and they'd often be much older than him. He'd connive to get off from many chores and often coerced his sisters to have them do his share. In addition, he was hardly around as he'd spend days on end with other Nikkei boys just plotting mischief and wasting time.

Agueda, the youngest, was often with Carmen as the latter was protective of her. She was pretty and quiet, and although Li'a' and I considered her to be reserved, she often spoke her mind without prejudice. Sometimes we'd encourage her to be a bit more assertive. She also showed profound impatience with people who weren't quick-witted. Agueda and Carmen often led the family prayers in times of strife. Agueda was also athletic and her favorite sport was baseball. In the early days of Guam, baseball was popular. Agueda was soon sought after by many teams, mostly made up of village boys, to play on their teams. She was a good pitcher and was quite known for scoring home runs as she was also good at hitting balls that went far beyond the field. As a father, I could never refer to her as a tomboy, but her athleticism told me otherwise despite her femininity.

It was safe to say that the issei, who traveled from Yokohama to Guam to work on the copra plantation, were in their teens. It was a yearly thing as the contract allowed by the U.S. Naval Administration was a calendar schedule that ran from February to the following February, year after year. Tåtan Kåcha only went to Tochigi, Ibaraki, and Gunma to recruit workers. Soon, many issei would see cousins and neighbors working for the plantation, and while many returned to Japan after fulfilling the year's contract, others stayed behind. Sometimes, there were returnees, men who had worked on the plantation years before and then decided to return. Those who were older sometimes left behind families in Japan, and when their year was up, they signed on to continue to work as they liked island life. They petitioned for their wives and children to come to Guam through Tåtan Kåcha. There were varying ages among the Nikkei community, year after year.

Soon, it became difficult to determine who was nisei or sansei and beyond. This distinction of determining generational numerical sequences became mired in confusion. Speculation stopped. By the approach of World War II, many nisei were still children, others were adults and having families, and even sansei were soon older than many nisei.

Much of this distinction depended solely on the issei for clarification, but by the time the war began, many of them became tightlipped. Some insisted that Japanese not be spoken in their families for fear of retribution, which included untold punishment and even death. The Japanese invaders were cruel and unforgiving for any slight offense.

I claimed the island of Guam as my home. I counted on my fingers about a few dozen men, issei, at best, who echoed my sentiments when we were gathered one day at the home of another issei in Matåguak. We were all married to local women and had children. A few were starting to have grandchildren. At the gathering, we realized that we were all speaking CHamoru, as if Japanese was now a figment of our imagination. Thank goodness, many wives learned Japanese from us when we first married. It was they who made it a point to teach our children their heritage and language.

In fact, on occasion, our wives would scold and lecture us about that particular lack of discipline. They made sure that we never forgot from where we came. They constantly told us to be proud of who we were, and that adopting

Guam and anything CHamoru was also a good thing. It didn't matter what our lot in life was. However, our Japanese ethnicity was to bear heavily on us during the war. Little did we know our destiny, too.

CHAPTER 13

The Community
ZENPEI

By the '30s, the copra industry was in full production mode. The island was enjoying prosperity. Contract workers came and went every year. Sometimes only a handful came, and other years, they came by the dozens. I didn't know that Tåtan Kåcha was allowed a yearly maximum of 100 contractual workers, nor did I know whether he ever reached the allotted number on any given year. The workers often were divided evenly to either Tokcha' or Hinapsan. Later, when Hinapsan closed and with the added shipments to Australia, I made sure manpower was at a maximum to meet the increased demands from the other markets.

At Tokcha, hired men wasted no time in learning everything about copra production. Our work was mostly uninterrupted, save for a few *taifuns* that wrought havoc on the plantation, but it always rebounded in due time. Many contract workers chose to fulfill the one-year contract and then renew. They confided that there was much comfort in the work conditions. There were few complaints.

Some married while still employed at the plantation and moved into the villages to start their families. Tåtan Kåcha recouped his losses from the Hinapsan closure, and business began booming in Hagåtña. Since I had taken over management at Tokcha', he rarely made an appearance unless for promotional celebrations and the annual Christmas bonus and party that was now held at the plantation. Thanksgiving, too, soon became a tradition as Mrs. Shimizu introduced the issei and their families to this annual feast that brought joy, friendship, and bonding. The turkeys that were miraculously part of our celebrations were imported from a place that was called Sacramento, California, and they arrived on a ship called the USS Supply, which brought over Guam's naval governors and their families. Somehow, the Shimizus rubbed elbows with the government's powers-that-be. The huge roasted poultry that graced our table was a highlight of our Thanksgiving for the years that we celebrated it. It wasn't long before our Thanksgiving celebrations consisted of two to three roasted turkeys, and nisei, sansei, in-laws, neighbors, and friends began joining in as invitees by a copra worker. There was one Thanksgiving when priests, who were from a number of the parish churches we attended, graced our gathering. In fact, in unison, they blessed the table. We were honored.

Some issei, despite not continuing a contract with the plantation, chose to stay on the island, found employment, settled down, and moved on with their lives. They never severed contact, friendship, and relations with the rest of the Nikkei community. Many issei spoke CHamoru fluently, adjusted to the culture and traditions, developed a devotion to the Catholic faith, and became fully entrenched in the local politics of the day.

Nikkei children enrolled in the school system at the time excelled especially in sports and academics. They became assimilated into the CHamoru community, went about their daily lives and were proud, obedient offspring of the Nikkei community. The children were involved in their churches, villages, ranches, and in the care of their elders. For the older set, politics, meaningful employment, romance, and soon, marriages ensued with others in their villages, not necessarily with other Nikkei, but with young men and women who were CHamoru or of other ethnic lineages such as Filipino, Chinese, German, Italian, Spanish, other Pacific islanders, and even statesiders. Life in Guam was blissful, harmonious, and pleasant. The third generation of sansei was also, by then, part of the island's social fabric.

Some issei still felt homesick, followed Buddhist rituals, and paid homage to their native land, but managed to live harmoniously among the Nikkei and CHamoru communities.

Others still had difficulty adjusting to the heat and humidity of the tropics. The flu season was often merciless. Some issei died, but they were given rites of extreme unction and buried in the scattered cemeteries on the island.

CHAPTER 14

The Issei Woman

ZENPEI

I do not engage in gossip. This was a policy I picked up from Tåtan Kåcha and his no-gossip policy in the plantation's operation. He frowned upon things that he thought were petty and unnecessary, which I liked because it saved me from unneeded anguish in the workplace. I applied the same policy when dealing with the Nikkei community. I figured that the less information is known about people, the better. It was only my wife to whom I'd speak to about such things. I trusted her because she didn't involve herself in such pastimes, whether within CHamoru or Nikkei communities. However, there was a woman of significant importance that I will speak about because she figured quite prominently during the Japanese occupation.

The ship known as Dai Ichi Tora Maru, owned by JK Shimizu, also went to and from Saipan, landed on Guam and continued to Yokohama. Many passengers were affluent CHamoru from both islands. Some disembarked at the port of call in Japan. It wasn't known if the ship also traveled beyond Tokyo to other outlying areas like Palau, or other Micronesian destinations, Hawai'i, or on to San Francisco.

According to the *Guam Newsletter*, the ship seemed to also have a different name as a few passages in the newsletter mentioned a Marianas Maru, owned also by JK Shimizu. It wasn't disclosed if Tåtan Kåcha owned only one ship or perhaps a fleet. The USS Supply brought cargo and passengers, mainly

U.S. Navy and U.S. Marine officers, the appointed governor, and his family members to and from Guam. Their names were listed on the passenger manifests, including gender and rank. Because Guam was a U.S. possession this far out in the Pacific, the USS Supply did not go to Saipan. Passengers from Saipan wanting to go to the U.S. mainland had to board a Maru to Guam, purchase route fare on the USS Supply, and sail to the United States.

Among the Maru's passengers from Yokohama was a woman, Masumi Sasakura, who came from Tokyo. It was said she arrived with lots of money. She was reportedly a *maiko*, a geisha who was popularly known throughout the city and was considered a woman of grace, beauty, and talent for the art of singing, dancing, playing the *samisen* and *koto*, flower arranging called *ikebana*, the ceremonial tea ritual, and calligraphy. In addition, she also knew the English language and was reputed to be very fluent.

She mastered all the facets of being a geisha as she began her training at the age of nine. By the time she was in her 20s, she was unrivaled in her position. She also was a sought-after performer in Kabuki, where she was one of the very few women performers past the decade of 1910. Because of her, she opened the door of opportunity for a few others who joined the ranks of performers. She ran an *ochaya*, a teahouse that was owned and sponsored by one of the city's most renowned but unscrupulous businessmen. He supplied the *ochaya* with additional lesser ranks of geisha, but also, on an almost daily and nightly basis, he brought scores of foreign diplomats and Japanese elite of all ranks, such as politicians, government leaders, and prefectural officials, to the *ochaya*. From her management of the *ochaya*, it wasn't any wonder that Ms. Sasakura knew the English language fluently.

The businessman who owned the *ochaya* was very rich. His businesses ranged from banking, restaurants, manufacturing, trade, shipping, and industrial goods. He also had homes in practically all the islands of Japan, from Hokkaido, Honshu, Shikoku, Kyushu to the Ryukyus, and Okinawa. Even I knew of him as a youngster while I was living in Oyama City, before I left for Guam. My parents and neighbors spoke of him often, and many were envious of his status in the country. I wouldn't be surprised if his name and his wealth appeared in tabloids all across the prefectures and Japan itself.

The businessman was caught in a deal to establish an *onsen* facility in one of the prefectures. *Onsen* are hot springs that are popular and frequented by many people, especially during the freezing winter.

The business deal apparently had a disastrous outcome, and millions of yen were reportedly lost in a money laundering scheme. The scam involved diplomats and businessmen who were apparently guided by Ms. Sasakura. The scandal brought tremendous ruination to reputations and standing in the prominent financial community.

Ms. Sasakura "lost face," and was shunned by the geisha community. She decided to flee the country by secretly selling her lavish home, which she had originally bought from her hard-earned wages and investments. She staged a disappearance. She abandoned her nearly 200 silk kimonos and all accessories by tying them to heavy stones and had her male assistants dump them into the murky waters off the bridge near the *ochaya* in downtown Tokyo. In the dead of night, one autumn, was the last that anyone ever saw her again.

Like me and many others from years before, she boarded the ship at Yokohama with a destination of wherever struck her fancy. The ship was headed to the outer Pacific, to places she'd never heard of before. The ship was the Marianas Maru. The only things she had in her possession were three bags of currency in yen that she had carefully wrapped with light, cotton, plain material. She dressed as a man, cut her hair short, covered her face and head with a wrap to disguise herself. She paid for a cabin on board and stayed there for the duration of travel through the seas.

She managed sea sickness, vomiting only in her cabin in a small container, knowing that the less she ate, the less she expelled from her stomach. She emptied the container into the sea, but only in the dead of night when passengers and crew were at rest. She maintained obscurity, only venturing forth for meals and an occasional, rare stroll on the ship, usually under the cover of night. So as not to draw attention to herself, she was clad shabbily in the same trousers and shirt for the whole two-week trip. She tried to appear like a man, but many of the passengers couldn't shake the impression that she was an effeminate Japanese man. She was left alone until the ship made its entry into Guam.

For some reason, she decided to disembark and stay. Her decision to stay probably came from snatches of conversation she heard among the young men on board. She learned that almost all of them came from the country-side of Japan. Few, if any, had ever visited Tokyo's flamboyant nightlife or the teahouses frequented by geishas and ladies of the night. During that voyage, she realized that her disguise would remain intact. With a huge Japanese com-munity already in Saipan, she decided not to risk going there. It was Guam where she ended up living the rest of her life. She was perhaps, the first female issei, if not, the only one, on the island.

She established a business, a retail one that brought in goods, fabric, sundries, toys, and candies to the island. With her wealth from the bundles she brought along, she managed to purchase a home in the midst of a bustling village in old Tamuneng.

Many CHamoru and nisei frequented her place of business, at first in Hagåtña, then in Tamuneng. Ms. Sasakura was said to be kind, gentle, and respectful. During the war, she gave Nikkei families money, merchandise, food, and clothing and never requested reciprocation. She was considered a friend and was trusted. She'd ply children with Japanese candy that she'd have imported to the island, as well as the many sweet drinks that were sold at her business, but for the Nikkei children, they were free. For Nikkei teenagers, once she found out whose children they were, she gave them similar treats and even lunch money for school.

Despite the long years she spent on Guam, Ms. Sasakura didn't learn the CHamoru language. She maintained her Buddhist beliefs and had a shrine in her place of business. She also wore what I and many of the elderly issei said was a wardrobe of summer kimonos, not the lavish ones, but simple and amenable to the tropics. From the few times I had chance meetings with her, she was indeed an attractive Japanese woman, and I'd detect a scent of what a nisei woman told me was lavender.

The information I had gleaned about Ms. Sasakura was shared with me by a nisei woman who knew English, spoke fluent Japanese, and had worked for Ms. Sasakura at both her stores. The nisei woman eventually owned a business of her own, and because she retailed the gunny sacks that were in huge demand for our copra shipment, she became a close confidant of mine. She and my wife Li'a' worked side by side when we opened our business in Hagåtña from the seed money that Tåtan Kåcha provided as a loan. Li'a' was confirmation godmother to her only daughter, a sansei who was also friends with my daughters, most especially Måme' or Carmen.

CHAPTER 15

The Other Issei, the Scoundrel
ZENPEI

Tun Battasåt Nakasone was prosperous. He had a business in Hagåtña, one of the first to succeed in the issei community. His wife was CHamoru and was thought to put on airs. A Catholic churchgoer, she was a little more giving in terms of church tithings. She helped whenever she wanted, but mostly only people she knew or was related to. In CHamoru, she was *otguyosa*, which translates to someone who is a snob.

I share this passage about Tun Battasåt Nakasone as his reputation was an open secret among us issei. I consider the information to be common knowledge that circulated among us who'd lived in Guam the longest. He, too, was a figure that must not be forgotten because he did so many things that were sometimes described as unfortunate and unforgivable. But to us, as the first generation of the Nikkei families, it was his evil nature that contributed to our self-exile and kept us away from the CHamoru community.

He didn't come by way of the copra plantation as I certainly didn't know him nor did the other contract workers. I couldn't tell whether he came from any of the three Japan prefectures or from Saipan like Tåtan Kåcha. I didn't know if he'd arrive before, after, or at the same time as Tåtan Kåcha. Speculation also was that he might have come from Hawai'i or California, which would have explained his lack of personal history on island. However, he spoke Japanese and CHamoru, which must have been cultivated early on in his life.

His use and knowledge of English, I surmised, was from the patronage of the U.S. military officials of his business in pre-war Guam. During the war, the Japanese military officers were regular patrons and used his business as an official meeting place.

One person described him as "a pillar of the community." He was involved in community non-profit organizations, Chamber of Commerce, Order of Saint Francis, Knights of Saint Sylvestre, Guam's Village Baseball League, Benevolent and Protective Order of the Elks, Jagatna Civil Club, Guam Dramatic Club, and the Christmas Seals Campaign. He was on the committee that planned the annual Guam Industrial Fair.

The only organization he didn't belong to was the Young Men's League of Guam, which began in 1917. Another organization, the Elk's Club, more appropriately named the Benevolent and Protective Order of the Elks, consisted of businessmen who refused to allow men of CHamoru descent to become members. Many of the Elk's members were statesiders and mixed foreigners who wouldn't allow their sons from CHamoru wives to become members. The Young Men's League of Guam was organized to respond to the Elk's Club edict. A YMLG member had to be CHamoru, speak CHamoru, and conduct themselves in the manner and tradition of a CHamoru. Sons of a CHamoru woman and a non-CHamoru could be members, but certainly not statesiders and foreigners living on Guam. As an issei, despite being fluent in CHamoru and married to a CHamoru woman, Tun Battasåt wasn't eligible for membership. He loathed the organization.

He was also instrumental in helping the candidacy of many politicians seeking a seat in the Guam Congress, an advisory body to the island's U.S. Naval governors. In pre-war Guam, the Popular and Territorial political parties drew interest and involvement within the CHamoru community.

Tun Battasåt also headed a Guam Boxing Commission that sponsored boxing matches in some of the villages.

Once, too, he sponsored a circus with all the pomp of the big tent including acrobats, little people, tightrope walkers, clowns, a carnival barker, sequined beauties, and other acts. There were also several animals, one of each kind, including an elephant, tiger, bear, camel, kangaroo, donkey, Galapagos tortoise, and llama. He brought several monkeys, horses, snakes, and other circus attractions to the island.

Both he and JK Shimizu were early business owners who set up shop in Hagåtña. They thrived during the '20s, '30s and early '40s. Their businesses advertised almost daily in the *Guam Newsletter* and the *Guam Recorder*.

Many liked Tun Battasåt and many despised him, particularly those of us from the Nikkei community. His loyalties were questionable — whether it was for the United States, Japan, or his home island of Guam — primarily guided by his personal or financial gain. He was handsome, shrewd, cunning, jovial but traitorous, and scheming. He delved into gossip and took delight in pleasing the powers that be, whomever they might be at the time. In a sense, he was a bit of a narcissist, and it was obvious to many that he secretly enjoyed attention. He was also a practicing Catholic.

His position in the community was solid as he had the money, the influence, and the wit. He played significant roles, many negative ones toward the Nikkei, whom I would like to say were "his people." Whenever there was an atrocity against a Nikkei during the war that included investigations, confrontations, conflicts, blame, shame, and torture, Tun Battasåt had something to do with it. His name was connected to misdeeds, mistrusts, and oftentimes, death to the innocent.

Many of the manåmko' would often mutter under their breath about him, *"satanås ayu na taotao, lao po'lo sa' ti mamaigo' si Yu'os,"* which meant "that man is Satan, but God doesn't sleep."

CHAPTER 16

Conflict
ZENPEI

By the 1930s, T. Shinohara's Jagatna Gas Kitchen restaurant was a popular place. Both locals and military officials regularly patronized the eating establishment. In those days it featured standard but reasonable menu items that boasted American dishes, including french fries, hamburgers, hot dogs, pickled items, cole slaw, and simple sandwiches.

The restaurant catered to the young at heart. Many school-aged children scraped together coins just to purchase a glass or a bottle of Coca-Cola. The place was airy, where the breeze wafted in and out, affording cool comfort and relaxation. It had an open and welcoming atmosphere.

It was also big, spacious, nicely furnished, and situated on the ground level, making the place accessible to everyone. There was a small meeting room and a conference room that also doubled as a banquet room with dancing space. It had a corner for orchestras and other instruments, including a grand piano. It was indeed a favored social place to be seen and to mingle in formal occasions.

For sophisticated patrons, adults as well as U.S. military soldiers and officials, the nighttime dinner was ala carte fare that included all sorts of steaks, pork chops, lamb chops, lobster, crab, fish, other seafood, and prime rib of beef. For some reason, mashed or baked potatoes, more than rice, seemed to be the preferred side dish of starch.

Soups, salads, and desserts were plentiful with many varieties that included assorted cakes, pies, doughnuts, and the much-loved *latiya*. Coffee, tea, milk, hot chocolate, Coca-Cola (there were no other flavored soft drinks), and beer and liquor were available. The beverages appealed to regular customers, whereas alcohol was the major purchase of soldiers and affluent older locals.

It was the American servicemen who brought news to the locals about the outside world. Both the *Guam Newsletter* and the *Guam Recorder* featured mostly articles dealing with naval governors and their families, who or how many soldiers were listed in travel manifests, news of a local nature, some feature stories, and advertisements of local businesses.

It was at the restaurant where news about the conflict in Germany was discussed. Information circulated about atrocities, cruelty, the banishment and killing of those of the Jewish faith, and the armed invasions of nearby countries such as Poland and others that I didn't know. Not only did I know nothing about the Jews or the Jewish faith, but I had no idea where Europe was located or what Germans and Nazis looked like.

Notorious names like Mussolini and Hitler were frequently uttered in conversation. They were called dictators. They were responsible for millions of lives killed, massacred, and conquered. It seemed so far away. I ignored the information and didn't join in on conversations. We had no connection to the conflict.

We knew that the United States was involved, and the president, Franklin D. Roosevelt (whom I didn't know either), was communicating with Winston Churchill from Great Britain, wherever that was, and that war was looming ahead. Of course, my unfamiliar knowledge of English, the outside world, and what war was didn't register in my mind.

Life continued on the island, and there were no worries. During the mid-'30s, I didn't think much about any thought-provoking matters. A few years later, talk shifted to what was happening in this part of the Pacific.

There was a conflict between Japan and the United States. I didn't understand the politics or the scholarly assessments that circulated in educated circles. Military jargon seemed to pervade many casual and informal exchanges among people who freely discussed the conflict.

One day, I happened to be at a grocery store when I heard a nearby shopper whisper something to a companion. They were CHamoru and appeared to be nearly my age, perhaps older. I didn't know them, but one man said to the other, *"CHapanes ayu na taotao, adahi hao,"* telling him that I was Japanese, and to watch out.

Unsure of what was happening, I just nodded politely and exited the store. Everywhere I went, people seemed to be whispering and gesturing in my direction. Of course, I was unaware of whatever news was circulating.

I was soon visited by Augusto Kiyuna, a young nisei, who asked me if I was aware that CHamoru were suddenly initiating boycotts of issei-owned businesses in Hagåtña. I didn't know about this until I was summoned by a messenger from Tåtan Kåcha who told me to report to a meeting.

At his house, I recognized some of the men I worked with and supervised at the plantation. There was Murakami, Okada, Ichihara, Akiyama, Ooka, Yamashita, Ige, and Iwatsu, along with many others. There were older sons of some of the issei who weren't able to attend due to other obligations. And there were women, too, wives and daughters. Everyone was talking at once. Some appeared to be fearful. Others looked worried. Some began wiping away tears. Then, Tåtan Kåcha began speaking.

He addressed us in CHamoru. He said there was big trouble in Japan. The country was expanding its imperial domain, and the emperor had targeted the Pacific as his area of concentration. He explained there were planned invasions of many of the islands, but he didn't know which ones. He couldn't tell us whether Guam would be included. He appeared unsure, but said he was only warning us of possible trouble with the CHamoru people. We didn't know what to make of this because we'd already immersed ourselves in the island, in religion, in marrying into the culture, and, in particular, in language and allegiance to our new way of life.

He then told us that we must prepare for war, and he knew that the United States would defend the island in every way possible. It was then that

I felt fear in the pit of my stomach. I could see the fear on many of the faces who were there with me. He told us to go on with our lives and try to appear as normal as possible, without giving any indication that we were worried or that we'd react to anything negative that was hurled our way.

Some of us already shared that we were feeling something from our wives' relatives and neighbors. He then told us to go on our way, but to be careful and to take care of our families.

We didn't know if Tåtan Kåcha's neighbors were watching us through closed curtains or lurking somewhere in their yards. When we left, we tried to appear jovial and casual. Many of us discussed the upcoming *fi'esta* of Sånta Marian Kåmalin. It was a normal conversation to have as everyone on the island was anticipating a huge celebration and *fi'esta* gatherings throughout Hagåtña. It was a tradition that I liked and was excited about. But, inwardly, our spirits were dampened.

Soon, wives began telling their issei husbands that their parents forbade siblings and grandchildren from visiting us and our families. Nikkei were being dis-invited to planned activities. Vital information that usually came up in informal discussions slowed, then stopped suddenly. Nikkei stopped being informed about even the slightest bit of news about sickness and deaths.

One day, my wife Li'a' sobbed that the fresh shrimp and octopus *kelaguin*, two separate bowls that our daughter Måme' made, were thrown into the garbage after she delivered them. It was to be a contribution to an upcoming Holy Eucharist celebration for a niece who was to receive the sacrament in the parish church. Måme' was told that it was possibly poisoned as now the Japs, as she'd heard it, were getting back at the people through devious means. Of course, my daughter didn't know what was happening. I intentionally did not share with my children what I had heard and feared. It was still something I didn't want to believe.

By 1940, a year before war came to the island, issei already had started to talk to their children and grandchildren. We shared that danger was coming, and the future was uncertain.

Nikkei households began to practice caution and, above all, to refrain from even an utterance of a Japanese word or phrase. Issei were strict about this for fear that it would bring untold anguish.

Soon, Nikkei children in the schools were subjected to all sorts of negative behavior in classrooms by CHamoru teachers and classmates. Taunts, ridicule, and pranks were leveled at them. Wives were ignored by parents, elders, siblings, former childhood friends, and godsiblings. Boys were not invited into sports activities. Young Nikkei girls were no longer informed about important church chores nor were they included in many tasks of church cleaning and maintenance.

Li'a' and I had our children stop going to school. We wanted them to avoid possible skirmishes, bullying, and even fighting. Our youngest, Då, had already gotten into fistfights with boys from her baseball team.

I wasn't informed about the building of the *pala påla* around the Hagåtña church, and neither was I included in the building of the arch that graced the entrances to the villages in both East Hagåtña and Anigua'. I partook in these chores nearly every year since I became a baptized Catholic. There were others like me who were shunned. Many of us issei tried to render the customary *man- nginge'*, kissing the back hand of the people and the elderly we respected, but they'd withdraw their hands or didn't extend them when we made an attempt.

It was difficult to tell which was gossip or rumor, as both were rampant in the community. Nikkei families sought discussions and private conversations only among the Nikkei community. Their activities roused suspicion, which brought on more gossip and rumors.

Then, the bombing in Sumai happened on that fateful morning that ushered in World War II. People were killed, many of whom I personally knew. Many of us felt panic and fear deep in our hearts. It was depressing and sad. Recitations of rosaries were earnest. Every household, CHamoru or Nikkei, asked for forgiveness and blessings from Divine Providence. No one knew what to do. Fleeing Hagåtña, which soon saw the arrival of marching enemy troops, was the first step we took. By then, it became evident that we weren't only invaded, but had been simultaneously shunned by the families into which we married.

It was then that Tun Battasåt Nakasone showed his true colors. It was reported in the Nikkei circle that he'd personally paid a visit to the commanding general of the imperial forces that invaded the island. He actually welcomed them with open arms. He was planning a special dinner and entertainment for the military commander, his subordinate officers, and important individuals.

In addition to Tun Battasåt welcoming the new rulers of the island, he took it upon himself to say that he would organize a group of Guam issei who would function as translators and interpreters for the convenience of the Japanese military. He didn't inform any of us. We wondered why he took the liberty of volunteering us without our consultation or agreement.

He later told us through his messenger that we were summoned by the military commanding general to attend a meeting of 25 issei that he aptly named. I was at the top of the list, second after Tåtan Kåcha. The meeting, of course, was to take place after the evening dinner at the Jagatna Gas Kitchen for the officials of the invading forces. He told us that the meeting was mandatory or else.

Then, the nightmare began.

PART THREE

CHAPTER 17

Nisei

JIRO'

I'm Jiro'. I was born on July 7, 1930. My mother was not yet 16 when she gave birth to me. Her youngest sister Agueda was 10 years old when I was born, so we were raised together. That same year there was a boon of nisei *famagu'on* (children). I was taken in by my grandparents and raised as theirs. Their only son, Juan, whom I called Uncle John, was 12 years old. I can't remember anything significant about him, except he was forever absent in the lives of my grandparents. He was also mischievous and always getting spanked with the *kuåtta* (dried cowtail).

Tåtan Dera', as I called my grandfather, called me Jiro'. In Japanese, it means the second son. My Uncle John never had a Japanese nickname so I was the one who got it. I don't know why. I didn't know if I was my grandpa's *kiridu* (favorite child), but he took me to work at the plantation. I was always by his side, even in the office where he worked, or out at sea, catching fish for our meals. He was the hardest working issei that I knew. He and my Nånan Dera' had a good relationship. They were always whispering to each other, and my Nånan Dera', as my cousins and I addressed our grandmother, was also very affectionate.

Mind you, I was, in the sequence of the Japanese count, supposed to be a sansei, but I grew up referred to as a nisei. Tåtan Dera' preferred it. Often I'd hear him correcting people when referring to me, telling them that I was a nisei, not a sansei. My first cousin, Saburo, Christian name Augusto, was the sansei as he was born in 1935, five years after me, and although we played and grew up together, my Tåtan Dera' distinguished me as nisei, never a sansei.

When he and Nåna took me to Mass, Agueda, whom I never called auntie, helped dress me in my Sunday best. Together, we were introduced to other families as Då and Jiro, never as aunt and nephew. My mother and my aunts, Carmen and Ana, sometimes came with us to Mass, but Då and I were often dismissed to play with the other nisei.

I was barely eight or nine years old when Tåta and Nåna discussed that there might possibly be war. I didn't know what that was. They and the other issei families talked among themselves. It was then that I began to notice the distancing of some of my Balitres and Chetton relatives. They started treating us differently, and Nåna too, noticed a tremendous change from her own siblings.

It was Tan Mo', a brother, who didn't show up with his family to my nåna's San Roke *finakpo' nubena* (novena ending followed by dinner). Everyone else came, Tan Ki', Nan Dede', Nan Låna', and Nan Susa with their families. That night after everyone had gone home, I found Nåna weeping. She found out that Tan Mo' told another sibling that he'd never go to that "Jap's house" for whatever reason. Jap was the word given to the issei, a shortened form of the word Japanese, but said in a scornful tone. I remember feeling shocked.

Tåta and Nåna were living in Hagåtña by then. I was about nine years old when I finally realized that Tåtan Dera' didn't work at the plantation full-time anymore, but he'd often go there when called by Tåtan Kåcha for some project. He, like many other issei who had been helped by Tåtan Kåcha, opened a business, a soda fountain, on the corner lot of the city.

My grandparents had moved from Tomhom where the rest of Nåna's siblings were living. Her mother, Nånan de Leonora, had died months before, and her father, Tan Juan, was now living with his maiden daughter, my grandaunt Nan Låna'. Tåta and Nånan Dera' frequented Tomhom. Their previous house was taken over by Nan Susa, her husband, and one daughter who had survived an illness that claimed the lives of her four other children. Nan Susa and Nan Lâna' sympathized with their sister, Nånan Dera'. Nan Dede' was living in Sinahåñña with her second husband and all her children from her first husband, so she was rarely a part of any worthwhile conversation in the immediate family. Of course, great-grandfather Tan Juan was kept out of the conversation because, in his old age, he didn't need any stressful information. He died not long before the Japanese military invaded Hagåtña through Sumai.

I was a responsible grandson in the eyes of Tåta and Nånan Dera'. I wish I could have said I grew up fast, but I found that both my grandparents allowed me to be a little boy and made me play with kids my own age. In time, they depended on me for many things. I didn't know why Uncle John didn't serve as an older brother, but he had a mind of his own. From what I remembered about him, he had a very quick tongue and showed tremendous disrespect to neighbors, elders, and relatives. I often saw Nånan Dera' wipe away tears of embarrassment and frustration.

Uncle John could be described as a juvenile delinquent. He loved to brag. He was a show-off and was known to be conceited. He'd lie about things when confronted face to face. His sisters, which included my mother, often accused him of stealing their money. He was extremely handsome. At the young age of 12 or 13, he already had a string of girlfriends as old as 15, 16, or 17. Nåna and Tåta couldn't depend on him, even if it was life or death. I knew then that he wasn't the kind of uncle that one looked up to. My grandparents considered him a tremendous disappointment.

Despite being young, I was the one who chopped wood for the outside stove, walking for miles carrying it over my shoulders from deep in the jungles of Sinahåñña or Tutuhan. I walked to the beach to fish with fishing gear of nets, rods, and reels; caught crabs when the full moon was high in the sky, as well as coconut crabs. I'd participate in the killing of pigs or hunting deer with a couple of my cousins, dig the pits, and watch our catch turn in the hot pit of burning *ifet* (hard and heavy wood). I laid out fresh deer meat between screens to dry in the hot sun. I shooed flies away from the screens with woven coconut leaf fans. I killed and plucked chickens, and learned how to clean them for soup cooked with vegetables and starches. I cleaned reef fish that I'd caught and prepared the coals for barbecuing. I helped Nåna and her daughters in the kitchen with grating coconuts and heavy kitchen work. I hauled heavy containers of seawater for the long process of making salt in our outdoor kitchen.

I plowed and toiled in the garden at our ranch.

I did many tasks, including building the outhouse at the back of the house and store in Hagåtña. I dug the pit for that outhouse, which was laborious, back-breaking work using a shovel. It took more than a couple of weeks to finish the task. Then, I built the tin-roofed, tin-sided walls with the assorted 2x4s I got from Palting's lumberyard. I finished the project on my 10th birthday. That evening, the family had a home-baked cake with candles for me to blow out. We had *fi'esta* food that everyone had cooked without my knowing. It was a nice surprise.

I rarely saw my mother. I don't remember much about her because she had been sent out as a servant or housemaid to affluent and rich CHamoru or issei families.

There was affluence among those people for whom my mother cleaned house, cooked, and laundered clothes. Many looked down on my mother. There were a scant few issei that gave allegiance to the Imperial Forces of the Rising Sun. Later, during the war, many wives of the Japanese officers would give my mother rice and choice meats as a token of their appreciation. By then, CHamoru, who once employed her, let her go as they saw her as "one of the enemy." The Japanese military didn't pay my mother for her services, but she brought home what was given to her by the wives. It helped sustain us in the leanest of times, especially when soldiers began pillaging both CHamoru and Nikkei families.

My Auntie Nena' was sent to help Nan Låna' care for my great-grandfather Tan Juan. After he died, she continued living with Nan Låna' until she married Uncle Felix Mesa. Auntie Måme' and Då had their share of responsibilities, but I was pretty much Då's charge during my childhood. Auntie Måme' often accompanied me to the beach, and while I fished, she caught octopus, which she was very good at.

One day, I caught Uncle John rummaging through my belongings in a box stored under my bed. He was startled when I suddenly rushed him as he was on his knees, and his head was underneath the skirt of the bed. I asked him what he was doing. He was 22 at the time, a young adult. I was just 10, and many elders, as well as older cousins, had given me money on my birthday. I placed these gifts in an old sock, which I kept tied in a knot and stored in a crack on the floorboards in the corner of my room. At that age, I was sharing bedrooms with Då. Apparently, Uncle John had already rummaged through Då's belongings as the pockets of his trousers were bulging with coins and currency. He told me that he was looking for confirmation documents, which he needed to present to a would-be employer who needed the document. Whatever it was, I didn't understand and had no inkling as to his employment possibilities, as Nånan Dera' once described him as irresponsible, shiftless, lacking common sense, and lazy.

Then, feeling obviously caught red-handed and without my stash, he stormed out of the room. His final words were, "na'lilisto hao sa' ti åpmam para u guaha gera." Make yourself ready, for there'll be war soon.

CHAPTER 18

News of War

JIRO'

I discerned that something was wrong, beginning with Tan Mo's actions against my Nånan Dera', his sister. There was an ugliness when close and distant relatives showed disdain in social settings. Suffice it to say that it was what occurred during the prelude to the war, which seemed to be just around the corner. Some families outright chased Nikkei from social activities such as birthdays, *finakpo' lisåyu* (ending of rosaries), *fi'estas*, and even weddings.

Tan Engracia Morita shared a story she remembered from her childhood. Her family was told to leave a *komplimento* (evening reception at a bride-to-be's home on the night before a morning nuptial) for their god-daughter. By then, word of the possible invasion of Japan was already taking a toll on the local populace. It was the bride's mother who publicly announced to the gathering of guests that all "Japs and their families aren't welcome in my house anymore. Therefore, those who are Japs must get out of my house immediately."

Without comment, Tan Engracia's parents gathered their children and made their way to the car. The family, watched by sympathetic guests, drove off in shock and complete bewilderment. What was forgotten was the tremendous gifts the family had given, including the killing of a cow, plates and trays of dessert, and liquor. These were considered obligatory for godparents to a godchild's wedding. It was sad. When the war ended, and Tan Engracia's parents died, there was not one word of forgiveness, apology, or sympathy that came from the godchild, spouse, or parents. The estrangement carries to this day.

Tan Julia Noriko Kobata shared her story from childhood. She was at school one day, when, without her knowledge, while she was writing at her desk, a girl seated behind her, urged by other girls, took out her scissors and cut Tan Julia's long, flowing hair to the back of her shoulders. At first, Tan Julia thought she had an immediate disease or unknown condition as she picked up the long locks from the floor. She burst into tears when she realized the CHamoru girls around her were laughing. She ran past her shocked teacher and out of her classroom, off the school campus, and never came back. She didn't even remember her school grade at the time. She never completed her education.

One young nisei mother who needed canned milk for her baby and a toddler was denied the credit despite pleading with the business owner. She asked for at least one can of evaporated milk because her husband's pay period wouldn't happen until the following week. According to Tan Emilia Ozone, the businessman just shook his head and eventually chased the poor young mother out of the store. Tan Emilia followed the woman, stopped her as she was crying, and spoke with her. Tan Emilia led her to another store down the street, where she herself paid for about four cans of milk, bread, and a carton of eggs and gave it to the young nisei mother. Grateful, the woman kept thanking Tan Emilia. After they parted company, Tan Emilia traced her way back to the first store. She stood there and asked why the businessman denied credit to the young mother. The business owner told Tan Emilia that all Japs must be put in their place; therefore, not allowing them to patronize his business was the best thing to do. Tan Emilia was shocked.

Even parents ignored daughters, nieces, and cousins who married issei men. There was a CHamoru-Filipina woman who was married to a nisei. She gave birth to her fourth child. Her parents didn't give their blessings and only one sister showed up at her home to lend a hand with her post-childbirth recovery. Unfortunately, her father never came around. During the war, he was recruited to build a landing field in Tiyan and was forced to work to the point of exhaustion, and died thereafter. Her mother bore a grudge against her and her husband, and never came around.

When her mother died, the woman bade farewell from a distance at the funeral. An uncle chased her away when she attempted to attend the services. She let go of the unfortunate circumstances and learned to live separately from them. The sister who helped her in her post-childbirth recovery was the only family member of 12 siblings who continued a relationship with her.

Indignities swept throughout the island. The Nikkei families found themselves alone. No one would come to their significant activities, including deaths in the Nikkei families or funerals. Relatives stayed away. It soon spread to the non-patronization of Issei-owned businesses in Hagåtña. Some CHamoru openly ridiculed and scorned the Nikkei families. Gossip, rumors, and exaggerated stories that were outright lies were regularly circulated. The Nikkei, however, continued attending church services and paid their respects when necessary but did not stick around to socialize. In general, they stayed away for fear of ridicule, name-calling, being ignored, and looked at with disgust. Nobody bothered to render Nikkei elderly the *mannginge'* (kissing of the hand of elders), a CHamoru custom that stretched back to the early Spanish colonial period.

The Nikkei commiserated among themselves and stuck together. When help was needed, they went to one another to seek assistance.

Most of the issei, by the '20s and '30s, had adapted the CHamoru culture, language, and the raising of families. Many became devoted Catholics. They encouraged their nisei children to be fluent in CHamoru and, in turn, as they grew up, the cycle of life continued as nisei began marrying and raising succeeding generations.

Within the Nikkei community, intermarriages, new-fangled notions, modern influences, fads, and fashions also impacted their lives.

By the time the '30s approached its end, the gossip that circulated among the Nikkei families about Ms. Sasakura's past had become common knowledge. The information came from none other than the businessman, Tun Battasåt Nakasone. He passed around the information that she was, indeed, a *maiko'* of geisha past. After disembarking from the ship that brought her to Guam, Ms.

Sasakura wasted no time in establishing a business in the middle of the capital city of Hagåtña. With wealth she never disclosed, Ms. Sasakura began importing Japanese-made products. Further, Tun Battasåt circulated the gossip that Ms. Sasakura became the mistress of another local businessman who was considered rich, unimposing, and another "pillar of the community," despite the fact that he was already married with children on the island. Ms. Sasakura's products came to the island by way of her purported lover, another choice bit of information offered by the community's scoundrel.

Tun Battasåt's true colors began to surface. Issei who had business relationships with him — merchants who sold sundries, canned goods, groceries, household items, simple hardware, undergarments, hairpieces, accessories, makeup and fashions — were suddenly denied wholesale credit for goods. He did the same to regular Nikkei customers who purchased items of necessity.

Ms. Sasakura, according to Tan Magdalena Matsuyama, was kind, generous, and not known to be temperamental. She was always calm and complimentary toward people, CHamoru or Nikkei. When Tan Magdalena told her what was being said about her, Ms. Sasakura only smiled, nodded her head, and said with genuine sincerity, "Tun Battasåt would stop at nothing to appear above board, wouldn't he?" Of course, Ms. Sasakura was fluent in English, possibly even more fluent than Nakasone. And she was a private person. Tan Magdalena, too, also spoke English as she too had a business in Hagåtña and was schooled in the language.

Ms. Sasakura endeared herself to both Chamoru and Nikkei. Her shop was busy daily. While parents and adults were busy browsing and purchasing items, she plied children with tiny toys and candy. If she knew of a birthday, marriage, or even death, she gave a monetary gift or *chenchule'*. Even after the war, she was loved by many.

The gossip was soon forgotten as the business of daily life and the looming possibility of war were on everyone's mind. The *Voice of America*, tabloids of significance, television, and other forms of broadcast, either print or electronic, hadn't yet made their way to Guam. The island had only a radio station that broadcasted for limited hours of the day. The only reliable form of media or news was the *Guam Newsletter*, which became the *Guam Recorder*. Even then, information from the outside world was slow in coming, and rumors ran the gamut of information or misinformation depending on how one looked at it.

At some point, people on the island who had relatives in Saipan were disseminating information because of Saipan's bustling Japanese community. While Guam's copra industry was thriving, so too was Saipan's production of sugar from its acres and acres of sugar cane fields. It had a small locomotive that helped increase production on the island.

Traveling to and from Saipan was frequent as other ships based in Yokohama or other areas of Japan regularly went there. Only the Dai Ichi Tora Maru or the Marianas Maru made periodic trips to Japan for goods, copra, transport of equipment or machinery, and merchandise. On occasion, the ships brought passengers, many of whom disembarked or unloaded on Guam before the ship headed off to Saipan. News of and about the possibility of war came more from the local people rather than from international news sources.

The threat of war in the mid-to-late 1930s became a feared possibility even among Guam's leaders as the military was not yet privy to the possibility of armed conflict with Japan. However, international news brought forth the conflict in Europe with Hitler's atrocities against Jews, the invasion of countries within their area, and the exploits of war on the European continent.

The most devastating of all gossip was the circulation of information as to who stood as the elites within the Nikkei community. Tun Battasåt compiled a list. He named all the Nikkei businessmen in Hagåtña, those who were generous in tithings with the parish churches, and people that he deemed to be leaders such as teachers, village commissioners, bankers, and the well-to-do. Commoners who didn't possess material wealth of any sort were not included on the list. Tun Battasåt claimed the Nikkei on the list would not be subjected to any form of wartime atrocities because they'd be loyal, steadfast, and foremost in their allegiance to the Imperial Forces of the country of their birth.

Even during pre-invasion speculation, Tun Battasåt already elicited fear and terror in the Nikkei community.

CHAPTER 19

Invasion

JIRO'

I forgot which day it was, but I remember that it was just before the Monday *fi'esta* of Sånta Marian Kåmalin. We were at home when the buzzing sound of planes overhead brought everyone into the streets of the barrios of Hagåtña. We looked up into the bright sky and watched as planes upon planes of the rising sun flew in formation overhead. Flames stretched underneath the wings of what someone described as fighter planes.

A *techa* (prayer leader) got down on her knees and began loudly reciting the *lisåyu*. Before long, everyone followed suit and began following the litanies of the holy rosary. We didn't know what to make of what we had seen. However, there was fear in everyone's heart. The unknown was suddenly before us. Before this day, we were tormented by the threat of war only in our minds. In my young heart, I didn't know what war was or what it was destined to bring.

That night in our home in San Antonio, neighbors and relatives from the villages, ranches, and settlements kept dropping by. All conversation was about the warplanes from Japan and why they had chosen to fly over us. There was much speculation, prediction, and uncertainty about everything before us. For us children, we were told just to be careful and to pray to God almighty and all the saints, especially to Sånta Marian Kåmalin. We all knew that this was the time when all children must obey our elders. It was not the time to ask questions.

That night, we went to sleep in our beds. Mothers from all over the barrios recited the rosary, too, from their beds. It was loud enough for every member of the family to respond, but it could also be heard next door as other households were also praying.

With caution, fear, and silence, we woke early, did our morning rituals, and prepared to go to Mass. It was a somber walk from our homes to the parish. The church began to fill fast. Talk that was usually loud, cheerful, and filled with gaiety, was subdued. Everyone made their way to pews where they genuflected and proceeded to recite momentary prayers of devotion with a plea not to bring war onto the people of Guam. The packed church was quiet, except for the organ and a few psalms sung before Bishop Olano's entrance, as well as the fluttering sounds of hand-held fans.

The Mass began with the entrances of other village parish priests, the church hierarchy proceeding in its traditional line, and the opening prayer of the bishop. Everyone responded obediently. For that morning, aside from the regular responses and singing, you could sense that there was an uneasiness in the congregation.

I wasn't an altar boy, so I sat obediently with Nåna and Tåtan Dera, my mother, and her sisters. I was near the end of a pew. Again, Uncle John wasn't there. As we were headed to church, I overheard Nåna ask him about going to church. He replied that he was going fishing with a bunch of boys. Nåna just frowned, shook her head and herded us out the door. Uncle John didn't appear to be readying himself with fishing gear. In the back of my mind, I wondered whether I had ever seen him fish, let alone with fishing equipment. I felt that he truly didn't know how.

It was immediately after the communion that we felt it. It began as a rumbling beneath the ground. At first, the sensation felt like pangs of hunger in the pit of our stomachs. Then, another followed quickly, then another. Questioning eyes crossed many of the parishioners' faces. Everyone was glancing at each other with similar questioning looks. The rumbling continued again. All eyes focused on the bishop as he didn't appear as if he had felt anything. It was clear that his attention was on the Mass at hand.

Then, we heard the familiar sound of planes overhead. Many glanced upward toward the church ceiling, still with questioning looks. It was then, and only then, that the Bishop also looked upwards. This time the rumbling sounds were loud and reverberated through the church walls, and gasps were heard throughout the building.

A line of men soon entered the church and made their way to the altar, where many of the church leaders were seated. The head of the group made a beeline for the first priest, and whispered in his ear, after which the priest nodded. He turned to the priest next to him, continuing the process until the priest nearest to the bishop rose and walked to the bishop, whispering the message from the group's leader. Looking alarmed, Bishop Olano, went to the altar and made his announcement. His voice was clear.

"Better go home now," he said and blessed the congregation. Everyone gasped in horror and talk ensued as people made their way out of the church. I heard people talk about going to Sumai to check on relatives and friends. Many were visibly crying. By then, the planes flying overhead stopped, and everyone hurried home.

Those who had stayed home from Mass, because they were preparing for the *fi'esta*, were told of what had happened. Food that had already been prepared or was ready to be cooked was transferred to containers, wrapped and covered, and prepared to be taken to homes and ranches, as heads of households announced that they must leave the barrios immediately.

From children to the elderly, households were a frenzy of activity. Soon, there was a line of vehicles, some *karabao* carts, and walkers, holding bundles and containers, heading out of the capital city. By late afternoon, the barrios were nearly empty save for families who were packing their valuables.

By nightfall, most of the homes were deserted.

I remember the day so clearly. It was Monday, December 8, 1941. I was only 11 years old. For the first time in my life, I felt fear in the pit of my stomach. It was indescribable. I dared not mention my fear, or I would be thought of as silly.

Immediately after the morning bombing of Sumai by the Japanese, the people didn't know what to make of this most traumatic moment in their lives. War was a totally new thing, and all everyone had on their minds was imminent death and destruction, not knowing what to do next. People relied on their wits, noting that the feast day of the island's patroness was now a day of infamy for Guam.

No one knew what the Japanese military looked like, and certainly, no one expected to actually see them in person. Troops started marching into the city from the seashore along the coastlines of Assan and Piti. The day was chaotic. Many residents fled on foot, some with *karabao*, and others who were fortunate, in vehicles of their own. All everyone had on their minds was to flee Hagåtña, as it was assumed that the village would most likely be breached first by the Japanese invaders in their conquest.

Some hoped that all this would come to pass, that it would be brief, and that God and the Blessed Virgin had everything under control. It was all surreal, and everyone, young and old, did not know what to expect.

I knew about guns because, the summer before, an uncle, a cousin of my mother, brought me and several cousins to shoot for deer and wild pigs at Urunao, on the northern tip of the island. While it was fun being with them because they enjoyed the outdoors, I didn't relish the thought of killing animals and carrying the heavy carcasses home. Of course, I didn't share my trepidation, but I kept thinking that the poor animals might have nursing fawns or piglets left behind to fend for themselves. Like humans, these poor animals' offspring waited in their dens to be fed; much like I would have been as a child waiting to get home to my family and a meal for me to eat.

Although the guns used in hunting were vastly different from guns used by men in combat, I knew they were the chief weapons used in times of war despite not fully knowing what war was like. In snatches of conversations between myself, relatives, and friends, we couldn't imagine what was to come but believed that death was imminent. The fear spared no one. It was scary enough, too, as it dawned on me that CHamoru, who once claimed to be relatives, neighbors, and former friends, now hated us and didn't trust us. Would they be the ones who'd pull the trigger against us? I was confused. My heart was scared as this fear became a recurring feeling.

Soon, abandoned homes and businesses in Hagåtña were established as the official headquarters of the invading forces. Soldiers' barracks and officers' quarters were set up; cooking, laundry, and commissary facilities sprung up. Soon after, recreation, physical training, dispensaries, post offices, ration acquisitions for the natives, and comfort homes for additional entertainment of the soldiers were established.

It wasn't long before the invasion brought on additional horrors. It began with the mandatory identification of the natives in the form of a square piece of fabric with vital information about an individual but written in Japanese characters. This was pinned to the outside shirt or blouse. Only infants were spared the identification fabric. Soon, former mom-and-pop stores were re-opened with soldiers in charge of distribution. These stores were once owned by issei or CHamoru merchants, and their merchandise was now at the occupying force's disposal without consent by the original owners. The soldiers began to distribute the merchandise as assigned food rations to families. After merchandise ran out, rice and whatever available canned goods that were brought in from Japan were distributed. Later, this system changed to food ration coupons when food became scarce between the rainy and hot, dry spells. Both CHamoru and Nikkei oftentimes stole these coupons when difficulty sustaining provisions nearly became epidemic.

Rules were established that required strict adherence. If not followed, punishment would be administered in the form of the *binta'*, or a slap on the face administered by anyone who was Japanese. The act of bowing when one comes face-to-face with any Japanese soldier was mandatory. The ultimate was to bow facing north, south, east, or west to the mythical god who was the emperor of Japan as instructed by a Japanese officer. This act of homage was deemed, by Japanese officials, an act of allegiance and reverence to the emperor and, most importantly, to the land of the rising sun.

As Nikkei, family patriarchs and families were required to be in attendance when called upon at a moment's notice, especially for the regular and plentiful parades and ceremonies, as well as the interrogations of people that often led to beheadings and burial in plots of dug graves. Nikkei also were required to provide food, vegetables, fruits, livestock, and seafood without compensation. Suffering, deprivation, and punishment soon became the trademark of the new rulers of the island.

Tåtan Dera' somehow managed to consult with Tåtan Kåcha about the war. Tåtan Kåcha, as I heard my grandfather relate to Nåna, was scared, too. He was tormented trying to soothe the fears of many of the issei under his employ, as well as former employees who were now fully entrenched with their lives in the villages. Considered by many issei as the *saina* (elder of the entire Nikkei community), he was sought after for advice, and everything that he had to say was taken to heart.

Tåtan Kåcha also gave our family permission to live in hiding at the Tokcha' plantation. He instructed Tåtan Dera' to destroy as many of the buildings and facilities there so the plantation would appear abandoned. Tåtan Dera' had all this mapped in his mind as he knew the plantation much better than anyone from the years of his employment there. We stayed there alone for the duration of the war.

The plantation was abandoned. Many workers who had been quartered there had moved to the many villages and assimilated with other families. Others were already married and had homes with their families. Others fled to outlying ranches and deep jungles to hide and fend for themselves.

For the first few weeks, we adjusted to life at Tokcha'. I had many chores, but late at night, under the cover of darkness, Då and I took turns patrolling the area in case of intruders. As instructed by Tåtan Dera', who was also instructed by Tåtan Kåcha — myself, Då', Auntie Måme', and my cousins Saburo and Shiro' took clubs, machetes, and other heavy tools to destroy the buildings on the plantation, in case marauding Japanese soldiers stumbled on to the property. It became unrecognizable after a while, and only our quarters remained decent.

Again, Uncle John was not around, and when he showed up, he'd linger for a while and then disappear for days on end. Every time he showed up, he was always ravenous and ate unceasingly at all hours of the day and into the night.

A nisei woman living in Yo'ña would visit regularly, always on foot. Tan Agripina Teranishi was younger than Nånan Dera', but they were godsisters. Nåna and Tåtan Dera' were the baptismal godparents to one of Tan Agripina's sons. From her home in Yo'ña, Tan Agripina brought us four egg-laying hens, seedlings for wing beans, okra, hot peppers, cucumbers, tomatoes, and bitter melon. She instructed my grandparents to plant the vegetables, scattered at random, giving the impression that they grew wild.

She later brought two goats that she said produced milk, as living in the village was becoming risky. News reached us that Japanese soldiers were now patrolling villages and nearby ranchlands for crops, cattle, or seafood. Her family and my grandparents exchanged whatever there was for survival such as fish, vegetables, fruits, and even crude cheese that Nånan Dera' somehow learned to make from the goats' milk. Tan Agripina and her family were about the only trusted Nikkei we could rely on during the war. During one particular heavy typhoon, Tan Agripina let us stay at her house during the storm.

The invasion changed everyone. One of the first things Japanese officials did was order a mandatory meeting for issei, who would be addressed by the chief commander of the invaders. Of course, Tun Battasåt wasted no time in welcoming them to Guam. I imagined he must have been a one-person welcoming committee. I'm sure he assured them that he was at their service. I wondered about the list of elites that he compiled. I wanted to know if he'd given it to the military officials. Word also circulated that he compiled another list of about 25 issei who spoke Japanese, knew the island well, and would be prime candidates for interpreters, as the mandatory meeting was to enlist them as interpreters for the invaders.

Tåtan Dera' was one of those summoned, along with others who were all friends, colleagues, and even godbrothers, as they'd been sponsors of a child's baptism or confirmation in the church. Heading the group was Tåtan Kåcha and the group of confidants that he had established a while back, as well as others who'd somehow appeared on the list that Tun Battasåt put together.

The 25 issei refused the request. However, it wasn't long before the price of the refusal was made clear. Interpreters were recruited from Saipan because of the refusal. I think they numbered around 10 initially. That was a turning point for many issei and their families.

None of the issei wanted to be a part of any plans for the Japanese military commanders. This disappointed and embarrassed Tun Battasåt. One of the military officers confided to him that the recruitment of translators from Saipan was costly. They needed to be brought over, housed, and fed — an expense that was to be borne by the Imperial Forces. It was then that Tun Battasåt must have decided that he'd wreak havoc on the Guam issei. He would make life as miserable as possible for the lot.

Only the issei and their immediate families knew of the betrayal of Tun Battasåt. His reputation as a traitor among the Nikkei was kept to themselves. By then, the Nikkei had learned to keep both distance and information away from others like the CHamoru, who, they believed, hated them just as much.

Tun Battasåt rendered friendship and assistance to the interpreters, with whom he'd collaborate on punishments for the uncooperative issei and their families. From then on, many Nikkei sought self-distancing and confinement away from both the CHamoru community and the Japanese conquerors.

A handful of Nikkei did services for the invaders, warranting special treatment and favors. They did not escape Tun Battasåt's scrutiny.

The scoundrel loomed in the background and listened to talk among the Nikkei. He then plotted and schemed and became the mouthpiece to the Japanese military leaders. They, in turn, established that Tun Battasåt's business was the meeting place of all the platoon leaders and high-ranking officers.

"People have changed," Tun Jacinto Rapolla said to some issei at a Matåguak ranch. It was one of several northern settlements that people fled to. Tun Jacinto didn't look nisei, as he had kinky hair, a dark complexion, and no telltale slanted eyes. His children, however, had the facial features. Tun Jacinto was one of the first nisei to change his surname at the beginning of the Japanese invasion, choosing instead to carry his wife's name as she was a CHamoru-Filipina by birth. He was spared confrontations and mandatory meetings with the invading forces. He, however, spoke fluent Japanese.

Tun Jacinto reminded everyone to always double-check to make sure we had our identification fabrics on ourselves, as many had difficulty remembering to wear them, especially children. This was to ensure that they would not be publicly reprimanded. Tun Florencio Yoshida, Tan Julia Noriko Kobata, Tun Luis Takimia, and Tun Takayoshi Okamitsu, had, on separate occasions, gotten their share of reprimands that were the repeated *binta*' across their faces.

Tun Jacinto said people in general became *hambiento* (greedy), *meskinu* (stingy), *sakke* (thieving), *taimamahlao* (shameless), *traidot* (traitorous), and *embidiosu* (envious). Sadder still, some people turned against each other and were privy to tattling, blaming, and participating in schemes of having people treated cruelly and punished intentionally by the invaders. Family members and relatives, near or distant, were guilty of this. Soon, the mistrust became more treacherous, if not dangerous. Throughout all of this, Tun Jacinto concluded that life on the island soon became a world full of fear of the unknown.

Tun Elias Ogawa Fejarang, a nisei whom I met in Long Beach, California, when I was much older, shared a tragic story about his brother and his young family living in Apotguan. An interpreter caught him rummaging through the trash can of the military compound on the northern edge of the village in Tamuneng, where he worked as a mess attendant. He was looking for pork skins that had been thrown out by cooks. As he was the one assigned to throw out the food, he'd carefully wrapped the skins in butcher paper with the intention of retrieving it later from the trash bin. He intended to cook the pork skins to feed his starving family. The interpreter reported his discovery to a commander who, in turn, divulged the information to Tun Battasåt. The man and his family, which included five small children, the youngest still an infant, and his young wife, disappeared from their home in Apotguan. No one knew where they were or whatever happened to them, but word got around that Tun Battasåt knew something. Tun Elias' family was torn apart by the mysterious disappearance of his brother and family. His parents and other siblings saved money and sold their possessions after the war to move to the States and lived there for the rest of their lives.

CHAPTER 20

The War Years

JIRO'

Tun Luis Takimia and I are the same age, and we both went to school together in Hagåtña. We often played marbles with our school chums. We kept our marbles in our desks to retrieve during recess or lunch time. I call him Tun, as well as others nearer my age or younger than me, out of respect.

Tun Luis Takimia's house in Assan was along the beach. He had seen several barges deposit soldiers in khaki uniforms and wielding bayonets inside the reef off Assan Beach. They spoke in familiar Japanese, a loud-voiced platoon commander ordered them ashore, and they waded onto the sandy shoreline. Tun Luis said they made a beeline to their right toward what he assumed was Sumai. The soldiers ignored the homes in Assan and Piti as their quest was perhaps to check on the bombardment leveled at Sumai starting in the area of Piti Harbor.

Tun Luis' family kept busy packing home essentials and burying important items in their yards. Once done, they fled their homestead. Neighbors followed suit by heading north, while others headed toward the island's central interior.

It was nightfall when the soldiers marched along the road from Sumai and headed to Hagåtña. Some dropped by several abandoned homes for drinking water and to prowl around looking for anyone or anything substantial.

Tun Luis was a nisei. During the war, we were just youngsters, but when he told me his story, we were already adults — he with a wife and two children. I was at his wedding. He was married at the Saint William's chapel in Tomhom. His wife was from there.

He said he was the last to leave his house. His parents and siblings left earlier. They walked toward Ma'ina. They had no vehicle to ride and decided to go to an aunt's family home further in the jungles between Tutuhan and Sinahånña. Tun Luis was tasked with bringing a heavy load, including pots, bedding, and other kitchen utensils that clanged and banged while he walked. He discarded them as they were too noisy. He found himself safe as he maneuvered his way in the twilight without his cargo.

Most of the time, he dove into dense undergrowth when he felt approaching platoons. He watched them carefully as they marched. There were about three to five platoons of men that he didn't bother to count. Making sure that the last soldier had marched off, he resumed his walk. He discovered nearly a dozen other men walking in his direction, as well as a young teenage girl, Clotilde Bayona, a CHamoru-Chinese-Filipina. The others varied in ages, young and old, from his village and from Tepungan in Piti. They were also escaping into the interior. With a sigh of relief, the group walked silently together on the trail that led them to their destinations. Some broke off and branched into other directions. Soon Luis found himself alone again on his way to his family.

Tun Antonio Akiyama, Tan Magdalena Matsuyama, Tan Katalina Maiyami, and Tun Bonifacio Suchida, in their mid-20s and 30s, were sent by their parents to Sumai to help whoever needed attention. They came from different households in areas like Fenna, the upper hills of Hågat, Sånta Cruz past Piti, and Mount Lamlam. Their parents saw the warplanes drop bombs and shoot from the air, and they watched the smoke that rose from the seaside village. Many had relatives who lived in Sumai, so all four, coming from different directions, converged on the paths and trails that led to Sumai.

The four didn't know each other, but Tun Bonifacio, whom I knew, told me at the Tutuhan stockade years later, that Sumai was a site of destruction as many homes and familiar terrain were either leveled or destroyed. Dwellings and commercial buildings were still smoldering with sparks and small fires amid black smoke that had overwhelmed the area. People from the village ran from their homes; some carried hastily put-together stretchers, as injured and bedridden people were carried into the streets, and the residents made their way on foot to trails and paths up the hills to Sånta Rita, Fenna, Hågat, and beyond.

People were hysterical. The four nisei helped carry toddlers and infants. Tun Antonio Akiyama carried an injured man on his back. It was Tan Katalina who confirmed that there were dead people carried from destroyed homes, and a couple of bodies were in the front yards of their houses. She didn't know how many had perished from the attack at Sumai. After the war, she wondered if those victims had ever been accounted for or properly buried.

It was horrific, according to Tun Bonifacio, who related that many people were dazed. Some were too hysterical to be calmed. One man punched his father-in-law into unconsciousness as his father-in-law was so unnerved that he had defecated and urinated on himself. He was simultaneously laughing and crying, while his wife and adult children were occupied helping other people in the village, many of whom were relatives from both sides of their family. Because of his mess, the wife stopped assisting an elderly aunt to be with her husband. According to the account, they were near the beach, and the poor woman had her sons drag their father into the water. It was there that he was washed and cleaned with seawater, while unconscious from the son-in-law's punch.

Soon, the atrocities began. Both CHamoru and Nikkei were subjected to mass announcements, which included instructions to go to some place, gather in a circle, and listen to interpreters as they verbalized additional orders given by commanders. The invaders' orders and instructions were difficult to understand, much less remember, and some were thought to be silly.

It was at these mass gatherings when children sneaked away to search for items that were either buried or left unattended in the yards of their homes, now occupied by the Imperial Forces. Parents instructed children to snatch things of value to bring back. According to Tan Agripina Teranishi, these were mostly documents like birth and marriage certificates, land deeds, and medical inoculation cards. Sometimes, hidden money was taken back to parents, too, when it was found. Tan Agripina didn't know if any of the youngsters were ever caught by the soldiers.

In the meantime, Nånan Dera' was trying to figure out Tåtan Dera' and my mother's secretive movements. My grandfather and mother would meet with other issei at all hours of the day or night. Sometimes, both didn't return until the wee hours of the night, and Nåna always made sure there was coffee and a hot meal waiting for them. Nåna stayed close to home and the store in Hagåtña. That soda fountain had closed by then.

Because of Tun Battasåt's treachery and intent to betray the Nikkei, word soon spread that the issei and nisei were not to be trusted. The family members of the Nikkei's CHamoru wives were the first to oblige. What had started before the war had gotten worse. Relatives, including parents, of the women who married these immigrants severed their relationships and contact. They stayed away. Nikkei families found themselves alone, to fend for themselves.

Issei were constantly on the alert. Many times, they were brought into custody and questioned about anything appearing wayward or perceived affronts to the Emperor of Japan, his dominions, the flag, and the courtesies of bowing. They were also questioned about any knowledge of George Tweed, the American GI whose whereabouts were continually sought during the war. The issei were slapped, beaten, kicked, ridiculed, and tortured beyond measure. A favorite form of torture was to have a garden hose run full blast at the back of their throats until their stomachs bloated. Some reportedly drowned and died.

Soon, older sansei, who'd reached the age of adulthood and with families of their own, began receiving similar mistreatment from the Japanese soldiers. It was learned that they were often corralled on the word of Tun Battasåt. His demands seemed to take precedence. Torture, massacre, and deaths of CHamoru and Nikkei came about because of Tun Battasåt.

Tan Katalina Maiyami sobbed at the story she shared of how she and relatives watched as three elderly issei were subjected to scrutiny about a gallon of tuba that turned into vinegar. The *tuba* was promised as a sweet alcoholic beverage to a ranking military commander. Because the commander didn't know about the stages of *tuba*, he automatically thought the men were trying to poison him with the fermented tuba. All three men tried to explain, but the commander just dismissed them altogether despite their use of Japanese. Tun Battasåt notified the commander that the three men conspired to put an end to his life. Tan Katalina and her companions watched as the men were beaten by a cowhide strap. One by one, the men bled to death in front of them while Tun Battasåt stood there, grinning from ear to ear.

Issei and their wives stayed awake late at night in their beds, sharing the day's happenings, such as who was tortured and suffered among the Nikkei. They kept the information to themselves. They refrained from sharing ordeals with their children or grandchildren for fear that they, too, would be subjected to harsh and cruel punishment by Japanese soldiers. The children themselves were already being subjected to cold shoulders and mistreatment by relatives who were once playmates and companions. In social situations, the children, were also subjected to ridicule and oftentimes beatings.

Without a country or people to feel some sense of community with, the Nikkei weren't spared any dignity. They were pillaged. Fruits and vegetables that they harvested didn't last long in their households because they were quickly snatched by marauding soldiers. Harvests from the ocean, too, were taken from them along with whatever livestock they had. There was poverty, famine, and illness everywhere in the CHamoru and Nikkei communities.

The interpreters and sympathizers were quick to pick up tidbits of information, and they'd inform Japanese officials often with added exaggeration or unfounded lies. I grew to hate them and avoided them at all costs. The heads of the Nikkei families warned everyone to stay away from them. When I was in their midst or was about to run into any of them, I'd reverse my route especially when in the company of other young Nikkei friends. We instinctively obeyed this instruction from our elders. We devised a plan where we'd scatter and walk in different directions but would converge at a known spot far away in our neighborhood.

Even among the locals, falsehoods were manufactured by certain people to inject some form of hope as the people's despair lay heavy. There was talk at one point about a transistor radio found in the jungle by some young boys, and it was passed around from person to person or family to family. The story was never substantiated, but word soon spread that the Americans would soon come to Guam, kill the Japanese, and free the island of the invaders.

Another news account shared that Tweed was found, the people who sheltered him were executed, and others were sent to Japan and imprisoned. The rumor also concluded that Tweed was beheaded.

There wasn't any substantiation to the rumors and gossip, but there were plenty and they came daily. Often, these gave people a false sense of hope. But the hope would give way when mistreatment, torture, beheadings, and massacres increased in frequency.

At one time, victory was declared along with the message that the Americans were finally on Guam. This was not true. The rumor lingered for a while, but stopped completely when marauding soldiers soon invaded ranch-lands and took whatever they found. Women, wives, and daughters were also molested in these instances. Soldiers severely beat anyone who attempted to stop them — children, young adults, and the elderly. It became hopeless after that.

The issei and nisei, too, wanted to believe the rumors of hope, but they continued to be shunned and ignored by everyone. There was fear and dread all the time.

Military commanders tasked lesser-ranked officers to pay visits to Nikkei families on the pretense of friendship and endearment, but the families knew better. They knew that everything that was said was often taken out of context. The interpreters went to the extent of feeding Tun Battasåt with their own version of tales. Tun Battasåt never gave or showed pity or consideration, as he took the position that not only were the Americans enemies, but so were local leaders, and the Nikkei were the lowest enemies of them all.

Soon, it became obvious when some Nikkei families began getting special treatment. We noticed that some did not wear the identification fabric. At a commissary store, a sansei child handed over a sheet of paper to the attending soldier, and she was given three, 10-pound bags of rice to bring home. Nikkei, standing in line along with CHamoru, had five pounds of rice poured onto a scale, and these were the rationed allotments. It didn't matter that there were huge families numbering anywhere from seven to a dozen or more. It appeared that some of the Nikkei were now kowtowing to the enemy.

Word spread that if Tun Battasåt came calling at a Nikkei's home, and if he asked a favor and it was given, chances were that the family would be exempted from unfavorable treatment. This was cause for concern for other Nikkei and alerted them to be more fervent in their precautionary measures — to be alert as many suspected that an ulterior motive brewed in Tun Battasåt's mind. Simultaneously, it was also seen that the special treatment did not last. If special treatment was granted, the next time around, it was back to the way it was — ridicule, discontent, and refusal.

As a result, Nikkei families carefully scrutinized others within their community and soon established connections only among those they could trust.

Able-bodied, pre-teen nisei were soon used as couriers, delivering parcels of raw food items, vegetables and fruits, medicinal concoctions like the *åmot tininu* (herbal liquid for flu symptoms), *pugua'* (betel nut), *åfok* (ground lime), *pupulu* (pepper leaves), *låñan manlassa* (massage oil), *dånges siha* (candles), *lateriha siha* (canned goods), *yåtdas magågu* (yardage), and *mensåhi siha* (messages) to and from homes in the outlying areas.

I, as the eldest of Nåna and Tåtan Dera's charge, was also recruited, together with my cousins Saburo and Shiro, to be a part of the courier group. However, we all worked separately. Sometimes in the darkness of night, the older ones, who were more adept at maneuvering in familiar jungle areas, would bring a younger one to train, maneuvering silently through difficult terrain and avoiding any possible racket that could stir the attention of the enemies lying in wait. During the day we'd traverse many areas picking medicinal plants, fallen coconuts, and even fruits like the *åtes* (sweet sop), *anonas* (custard apple), *hutu* (seedling breadfruit), *åbas* (wild guava), and *pi'ot* (sour seeds). Every once in a while, we'd be in luck and bring home bunches of cooking bananas from trees that were left abandoned at some outlying ranch. Pre-teens and teen-agers between the ages of 12 and 17 were often tasked with carrying heavy loads of items such as tools and small equipment to deliver. Once Shiro carried a *kåmyo* (coconut grater) to an elderly man.

The system worked. It was a careful system whereby the pre-teens and teen-agers worked alone and established their own routes, choosing never to walk the same paths as before. Because they moved quickly and quietly, day or night, communication between Nikkei families was kept from Tun Battasåt, the interpreters, sympathizers, and would-be traitors. This was an underground railroad that never ceased. Word circulated among the Nikkei that many pre-teens and teen-agers, boys and girls, knew how to recite the rosary in CHamoru. Many times, these young individuals came to homes and recited nightly rosaries, especially during the Christmas season when the *promesa* (heavenly promise) novena was said for the *Nubenan Niño Jesus* or the devotional prayer for the Christ Child. The same also applied to Sånta Marian Kåmalin that was traditional and ended on December 8, which had been the start of World War II on Guam. Religious Christmas hymns were not sung but families resorted to just softly reciting them.

One pre-teen claimed to have run into Påle' Jesus Baza Duenas. Word leaked to the CHamoru that novenas were being conducted. Not one Nikkei admitted to such activity. Again, only those near, dear, and trusted were a part of the courier system. Further, not one courier reported running into marauding Japanese soldiers. Working alone was another advantage of the underground railroad.

The patriarchs who initially refused to interpret for the Japanese military were often summoned to answer accusations leveled against them or to substantiate untruths. These sessions often involved beatings. Late at night, the issei spoke softly to their wives in CHamoru, avoiding the listening ears of their children for fear that they, too, would be subjected to cruel punishment if they were to be forced to talk against their parents. The fear of losing a child was always present in their minds.

I discovered that Tåtan Dera' was, on more than one occasion, interrogated by the commanding general. When word of these tortures circulated among the Nikkei community, I asked Tåta and Nåna if this was true, and if

Tåta was ever subjected to such an ordeal. It took a while for him to admit it, as Nåna gave him an encouraging nod to go ahead and share this bit of information. They both knew I could be trusted. He hesitantly said it happened three times, twice with Tåtan Kåcha. He didn't disclose what was said during his or Tåtan Kåcha's interrogations, didn't deny the severe punishment he experienced, but didn't disclose how the punishment was carried out either.

I was furious at the Japanese for what they did to my Tåta. I harbored deep in my heart such hatred, but Nåna cautioned me that I must look to God and hand over my feelings of disgust to him because, no matter what, God will find the answer. The whole time, Tåta talked about his experience, he never looked me in the eyes. I thought he felt ashamed, and I didn't comment further.

When the war was nearing its end, the CHamoru community was forced to walk to Manenggon and be confined there, but the Nikkei was not. No one explained why the Nikkei wasn't included. It was surmised that, because they lived almost anonymously in deep jungles, ranches that were difficult to access, and other unfamiliar areas, they either did not know or were left alone. In truth, many of the Nikkei were the last to know that the war had ended, although fully aware of the intense bombardment, shelling, explosions, and exchanges of gunfire between the Japanese and the U.S. Marines. With the intense shelling overhead, the Nikkei did everything they could to stay safe, from hiding in caves and cavernous outcrops of terrain, heavily wooded areas, in holes underneath their dwelling, between rocky cliffs, and huddled en masse in whatever confined spaces they thought were safe.

Because the issei and their families were already scorned by the Imperial forces, as the Japanese saw them as inferior through their bloodlines — their mistreatment proved this — no one supported the notion that the issei collaborated with the enemy except for Tun Battaåt Nakasone. No one could substantiate whether he and others were deported to Japan after the United States recaptured the island, or that the United States had anything to do with deporting them. It was Japan's Imperial Forces who transferred and confined U.S. military captives, American citizens on the island, anyone appearing to have Caucasian features, like Bishop Olano, and others of distinction or notoriety, to Japan as prisoners-of-war.

CHAPTER 21

Tåtan Kåcha

JIRO'

As a child, it was bad manners for children to engage in conversation with older people, even if they were siblings, and definitely not with the elderly. Our strict instruction was to render the custom of *mannginge'* (kissing of the hand) to elders, people of authority, and even the religious sectors of the community like priests and the bishop. Nuns and convents were non-existent while growing up and didn't come into existence until long after the war, maybe even post-Organic Act. Nevertheless, we'd be scolded, screamed at, or even spanked if we failed to render this act of respect. I was obedient. Many children hated attending rosaries, funerals, and social events. We would have to forge a line in front of seated people and go from person to person to render this gesture of respect.

That's why I'm offering my own perspective of Tåtan Kåcha. Although I saw him many times, especially at the plantation or when Tåta or Nånan Dera' took me to the store he owned in Hagåtña, I never had a moment to converse with him. I definitely had to render the *mannginge'* to him, his wife, and even some of the store clerks and cashiers who worked for him. Children spoke when spoken to and were forbidden to even look an elder in the eyes and attempt a conversation.

I'd see Tåtan Kåcha often as I'd be with Tåta at his job at the copra plantation, where I would be by his side daily and sometimes at night, too. After paying my respects, I'd disappear or stay seated, as sometimes both of them would task me to fetch or do some menial task nearby.

Sometimes Tåtan Kåcha would give me a small toy or candy from his store, for which I'd acknowledge and thank him. A few times, he'd run his hands over the hair on my head in a fatherly way. He'd compliment me to Tåta, saying I was well-mannered and respectful. A few times, too, he'd embrace me by kneeling down to my level and hugging me.

When I played with other children, I'd pass on tidbits of information about Tåtan Kåcha and how I'd see him constantly. Most of my companions were envious because they knew of him. He was regarded with great respect by their parents, siblings, and relatives. I often detected jealousy from my chums when I'd share that sometimes he gave me nice things from his store.

No one could claim that Tåtan Kåcha and his wife were godparents to anyone, including me. Tun Agusto Kiyuna, despite being my age and one of my boyhood companions, told me when we were adults that he'd overheard his parents discuss Tåtan Kåcha. He shared that Tåtan Kåcha was kind and took care of the plantation workers. Tun Agusto said his parents wanted the *saina* (revered elderly) to be his godfather for baptism, but Tåtan Kåcha had adopted a policy of not taking on that role because he felt that once he became a godfather to one child, many others would follow. He refrained from this practice and instead concentrated on being generous and helpful.

I never asked my Tåta if this was true. He said Tåtan Kåcha was instrumental in helping many issei who wanted to start businesses by providing seed money as a startup, and he didn't charge interest. Once the issei's venture was successful, they could begin paying him back.

A number of Tåtan Kåcha's grandsons and granddaughters were around my age, and they became fast friends as I'd see them often at the plantation's Christmas parties or at Mass.

I also saw similarities between Tåtan Dera' and Tåtan Kåcha. I marveled that their friendship was deep and long-lasting. Tåtan Kåcha was assertive, kind, and considerate. I never heard people mention that he was anything but those qualities. He, as per my Tåtan Dera', didn't engage in name bashing or outright denigration of anyone. He always looked at the good side of the men who worked at the plantation. Further, he wasn't known to lie, engage in gossip, or spend worthless moments speaking ill of people, including Tun Battasåt, who was the one who spent time talking badly about him. If anything, Tåtan Kåcha avoided Tun Battasåt even in social situations like church, community events, and programs. Tåtan Kåcha wasn't involved in organizations as a member or official, but rather, he would contribute in-kind or with funds.

It was for this reason that he was held in high regard by Nikkei and their families. If anything, he'd assist them with sometimes monetary help in times of crisis. He wasn't known to expect prompt reciprocation or demand payment for services that he rendered. He was patient, and people who owed him paid him when they were able to. Sometimes it took years before a borrower was able to pay him back. My Tåtan Dera' was also like that. I guess Tåtan Kåcha recognized that in him, as at the height of the war, my grandfather served as his right hand. For that, I also grew to love Tåtan Kåcha.

Tåtan Kåcha's legacy to the island of Guam was that he was bestowed the honor of being the Marianas Coconut King and was widely known for his enterprise. In the mid–1980s or perhaps the '90s, a Japanese woman researcher named Wakako Higuchi wrote a book about the Greater East Asia Co-Prosperity Sphere (GEACPS) and included the history of the Japanese military in this part of the Pacific. She made mention of Tåtan Kåcha's distinction. It is a fitting posthumous honor.

Of credit to his legacy, it must also be noted that his grandson, Frank Shimizu, corporate head of Ambros, Inc., and long-time board chair of the Guam Nikkei Association, was also honored with the Order of the Rising Sun, Silver Rays Decoration that was coordinated by the Ministry of Foreign Affairs of Japan (MOFA) and the officials of the Japan Consulate Office on Guam.

CHAPTER 22

Sumai
JIRO'

Before the war, the capital boasted a booming population. Families lived in harmony with their neighbors. People generally regarded each other as equals. There was no discrimination exhibited among them, especially among those who were Filipino, Chinese, Italian, German, and even others who moved to Guam from the neighboring islands of Saipan, Rota, Tinian, and Palau. The four islands were administered post-war by the Trust Territory of the Pacific Islands (TTPI) mandate in 1947.

The TTPI was established by the United Nations and administered by the United States during the period of 1947 to 1994. The TTPI encompassed three regions of Micronesia: the Marianas, except Guam; the Caroline Islands; and the Marshall Islands. Because the Marshalls were closer to Hawai'i, there weren't Marshallese who moved to Guam. The Catholic Church's census count made no mention of them, unlike citizens who came from Saipan, Rota, Tinian, and Palau.

Rivaling the capital city of Hagåtña was the coastal village of Sumai. Its history dates to the Spanish colonial period. The village remained ideal for the CHamoru inhabitants, who fished the nearby deep blue waters, farmed on its fertile grounds, and worshipped at the village church, where religious rites were the order of the day. A nearby cemetery boasted names of people who died from as far back as the early and mid-1800s.

I barely remember Sumai, as I only went there whenever Mass was held at its church. Both Nåna and Tåtan Dera' would take Då and me to the church services around that time. My great-grandmother, Nånan Leonora, was born and raised there. She had already died, not long before Tan Juan, her husband and my great-grandfather, whom I remember. He died just before the bombing of Sumai. There were relatives there from the Galaide' family roots, but I had lost track of them after the war. Later, I established contact and communication with some descendants who moved to Sånta Rita and remembered me.

The Trans-Pacific Cable Company was established in Sumai in 1903, linking Guam with both Asia and the United States. While Hagåtña had a thriving business community, Sumai had the advantage of nearby Åpla, which was the port of call for ships bringing consumable goods, machinery and equipment, merchandise, automobiles on rare occasions, and heavy vehicles such as busses, tractors, forklifts, and trucks. This was also the port of entry for JK Shimizu's ships, as well as the USS Supply coming from the States. The Dai Ichi Tora Maru, the Marianas Maru, and other ships from the surrounding islands came in regularly and brought imported goods, passengers, and other commodities.

On October 13, 1935, Pan American World Airways' seaplane made its landing in the waters of Åpla', perhaps as an unforeseen prelude to the island's tourism industry. Although that initial landing helped usher in the building of the Pan American World Airways in Sumai, the first of its kind for the island. It also established the airline's route of international flights. Pan American began hiring CHamoru to work as airline crews in those days. One famous pilot who flew in on that initial flight was Fred Noonan, the pilot who flew with Amelia Earhart on her transatlantic flight, which ended with her disappearance. Much later, another famous passenger was Ernest Hemingway.

The hotel in Sumai was a favorite gathering place of Guam's businessmen and political leaders, rivaling the Jagatna Gas Kitchen owned by T. Shinohara. Both businesses competed and had their share of robust daily earnings. The hotel, however, had a far better appeal as the island's elite had a firsthand chance to see international passengers, mingle with them, and get a glimpse of affluent travel. The first passenger service for Guam to nearby destinations, including the United States began on October 21, 1936, a year after it initially landed in Apra Harbor.

A power plant, other businesses, and various ventures were also in Sumai. In its midst was a bustling village of residents who worked, ranched, and plied their trades in the village that became no more when it was bombed by the Japanese.

Former residents were diverted to build homes in the hills of Sånta Rita where many descendants now live. Sumai became a part of the U.S. Naval Station and has remained off-limits for leisure visits, fishing, or hunting to the native civilian population since the war. Sumai was also wiped off the face of island maps, remembered only by descendants and islanders who knew its history. Once a year in the summer, around the time of Liberation Day, former residents are allowed into the military base for a Sunday of religious celebration, feasting, and paying homage at the Sumai cemetery.

There were few issei families that lived in Sumai, two of whom were the Noda and Tanaka clans that eventually were domiciled in Sånta Rita. A few graves appear to bear the names of issei, such as Sosoko, Matsunaga, Kamo, and an Iseyaki. Although many of the gravestones have been obliterated through age and exposure to the elements, it was assumed that the graves must be from the period of the 1800s until about 1940, based on the scattered, but still readable information left among crumbling gravestones. It can be assumed, too, that some issei must have settled in Sumai in the mid-1900s upon completion of their contract year at the copra plantation.

Many elderly who are still living today, beam with pride as they recall life in the village. Like Hagåtña, Sumai had the makings of a capital city. It had many great features beyond its harbor that brought in commercial transportation in shipping and the Pan American World Airways. It also had deep-sea fishing and perhaps a possible enterprise in commercial fishing for tuna. The soil was rich. It was surrounded by plentiful wildlife. Its surrounding areas were comprised of savannahs, a mountainous stretch with the main feature of Mt. Lamlam nearby, deep jungles, and the rich mangrove swamps and marshy areas that allowed the planting and harvesting of rice, the island's major starch crop.

Business boomed and commerce thrived in the village. People, too, lived in harmony and peace. Everyone, young or old, villagers and business owners together, along with the Catholic church, fostered a togetherness that accentuated the personality of the village.

Unfortunately, it ceased abruptly with the bombing of World War II.

CHAPTER 23

The Japanese Soldiers
JIRO'

As a toddler up until age 10, I didn't know I had Japanese blood. Although my mother and her siblings spoke Japanese, I never heard them converse. As children, because of our strict upbringing, we were expected to disappear whenever adults were conversing, which was often. This was a cardinal rule among all local children, and we obeyed it religiously. I spoke CHamoru and this was the language that Nåna and Tåtan Dera' spoke, too. Sure, I picked up on Japanese words, but this was evident even in the neighborhood of CHamoru or Nikkei children and others.

I became privy to the threat of being Japanese through school and during the war, which was scary when hearing it from older neighbors, my aunts and uncles, and my grandparents. It was during this time that Då told me that she and I were of Japanese blood as well as the rest of the family. Although Tåtan Dera' nicknamed me and my cousins with Japanese names, he never once uttered a word of Japanese and my cousins and I always thought our nicknames were CHamoru. We never questioned it. When accompanying him to his work at Tokcha' and Tåtan Kåcha was with him, I don't remember hearing them speak in any other language but CHamoru. English was definitely absent in my young life, including my years of schooling.

Therefore, my initial thoughts of the Japanese race were that they would look like bogeymen as I didn't think I'd ever known one, or was connected to one. Little did I know, they didn't look too different from me. Because I spoke very little English, CHamoru mostly, and a bit of Japanese that I picked up from my elders, being part CHapanes was what I knew as a word that described me and the Nikkei. I then learned the words Hapones and Niponges from one of the interpreters. I realized the words described the same thing, Japanese.

Aside from invading the island in their brown khaki uniforms and wielding guns with attached bayonets, they were not any different from me, other Nikkei, or even CHamoru. At first, the soldiers kept their distance, perhaps because of our language difference, and maybe because neither side knew English. Between the very little English that the soldiers knew, which was so ridiculously mispronounced, and the very little that the CHamoru spoke, with their strong accents, communication between the natives of Guam and the Japanese invaders was anything but adequate, much less comfortable.

A Japanese soldier was never alone. Four to five of them would be assigned to patrol or to command an activity or a project. If there were a dozen or more, they had an orderly system where everything was done in succession and usually at the command of a designated higher-ranked leader. There was always someone barking orders, and others would respond with a *hai*, which meant "yes" to anything and everything.

As natives, this was one of the first things we learned. We responded with a *hai* every time they spoke, even though we had no idea what was being said to us or whether those demands and requests were directed at us. If we didn't obey, we'd get slapped on either our right or left cheeks. We often anticipated the *binta*' because the soldiers administered it quite often.

I could not say that kindness was exhibited by the Japanese soldiers. We learned early on that they took whatever they saw on our people. They didn't ask. They were quick to slap us if we didn't bow to them. Sometimes, people would U-turn in their walk when they would see a soldier or two walking toward them. By the same token, the soldiers never offered anything, from candy, chewing gum, a cigarette, or a handshake. We always had to bow, and we soon learned to say thank you in their language even though we had nothing to be thankful for.

Parades happened frequently and at certain times, daily. I'm sure that it was their commander or some officer who planned, conducted, organized, and oversaw the staging of these parades in downtown Hagåtña. It was there where we saw colorful kimonos worn by wives of Japanese soldiers and what we thought were geishas, but they were actually ladies of the night. I also learned about the Monday ladies but that will be explained later.

The soldiers in uniform marched in unison on the days of parades. There were many of them. Sometimes a platoon was not assigned to participate, but they were often clad in loincloth and carried a heavy shrine called *omikoshi*. To my recollection, the *omikoshi* was usually at the beginning of the parade, but during certain parades, it would bring up the rear. I soon learned that it coincided with some sort of festival happening somewhere in Japan where the emperor was an honored guest. The military commanders' show of reverence was reflected in our local parades that were in homage to their leader. They chanted in their language and stopped momentarily in front of a grandstand where dignitaries of the day sat and applauded. Sometimes a designated head of a parade group would walk up to the dignitaries and hand them gifts. They then proceeded on, usually at the urging of another assigned leader.

The parade audience was comprised of the Nikkei families, personnel, staff, and families of the soldiers stationed in Guam. Included in the audience were a few CHamoru, Nikkei, and local children who were mandated to attend Japanese language school in downtown Hagåtña. There were dozens of these children. Very few CHamoru were present unless their attendance was demanded. As for the Nikkei, they were required to watch, or else punishment was meted. Japanese military wives demanded that the parades be held early in the morning or at dusk. It appeared that the heavy silk kimonos and accessories were not suitable for the island's humid and tropical weather, and, because rain showers were frequent at all times of the day or night, colorful, brilliantly painted parasols made of paper broke apart when wet.

The Nikkei families were often told at a moment's notice to report to Hagåtña whenever a parade was scheduled. It was at one of these parades that my family had a most unnerving shock.

The parade was not the only activity where Nikkei families were summoned. They also were summoned to witness beheadings, and while the parades were supposed to be merry, beheadings were not. The families were instructed to always applaud with masked expressions of joy, while deep inside they were remorseful, sad, in despair, and sorrowed. These two types of events happened frequently enough, and it became quite common that many in the Nikkei families just became zombies masking their feelings of disgust and hate for the people who claimed to be their countrymen. Only one man appeared to enjoy his status, power, and significance during that period, and that was Tun Battasåt. Often, Tun Battasåt was in the grandstand, which further disgusted the Nikkei. During one parade, he was there again but not in the grandstand.

I mentioned that my Uncle John was a frequently absent son. He was always into shenanigans of sorts. As an adult, now age 25 in 1943, he began hanging around with a bunch of other nisei near his age. He and his companions were ill-regarded by other people, including former neighborhood chums, peers, siblings, and even cousins. He and his companions were often absent in their respective family activities.

Imagine my family's shock when Uncle John, along with his companions of four other nisei young men, were accompanied at the rear of a parade by Tun Battasåt. They were the featured parade attraction as they walked the route, carrying a large U.S. flag. In front of the grandstand, dignitaries quietly watched as they stopped, spread the flag on the ground, and, in unison, began stomping and rolling around on the flag while simultaneously humming the U.S. national anthem as loud as they could. Uncle John, the showoff that he was, did somersaults and cartwheels and even walked in a handstand from one end of the flag to the other. The dignitaries smiled, cheered, and applauded in appreciation of this gesture of disrespect. Tun Battasåt, dressed in virgin-white long pants, a long-sleeved shirt, matching white shoes, and a tie emblazoned with the rising sun and its familiar red flames, stood proudly behind the boys with a huge smile. With outstretched arms, he gestured to the grandstand, as if presenting the finest of the Nikkei sons that the island had to offer. The Nikkei families quietly watched in shock and horror not knowing what to do.

Nånan Dera', in her embarrassment standing beside Tåtan Dera' who looked at the ground instead of his son, shed tears of shame at this show of disrespect. Then Nånan Dera' and the mothers of the other boys screamed loudly at their sons to stop what they were doing. Their screams soon drowned the applause at the grandstand. Uniformed soldiers appeared out of nowhere and screamed back at the women while walking toward them. The soldiers were screaming in the best English that they knew, then ended their scolding when they were right beside the women. The soldiers slapped the women across their cheeks. The women quieted, but sniffles and swallowed sobs began. Issei husbands held on to their wives in support. Then, everyone grew silent. The dignitaries at the bandstand stared back at the Nikkei families, and parade participants stood still. The Nikkei boys, in shock at seeing their mothers slapped before their very eyes, broke rank and ran into the jungle, leaving Tun Battasåt bewildered as he rolled up the flag, glanced into the jungle thinking or hoping that the boys would return, and resumed the parade, marching off into its conclusion.

CHAPTER 24

The Deaths of Issei

JIRO'

There is a sad note that must be shared here. Tan Magdalena Matsuyama shared the following information because she was tremendously affected by what had transpired. In chilling detail, she tearfully told me of what she knew about the whereabouts of the issei who perished toward the close of the war.

Tan Magdalena is a year younger than me. She was part of the youthful courier railroad group that I talked about earlier, in which my two cousins and I were involved. She also served as a *techa* in the courier group. We'd meet at intervals whenever the group leader convened to send us off to assigned Nikkei homes in the various outskirts of villages, usually in jungle areas where ranches and hideaways were scattered. I knew her as Mag, but a lot of people called her Maggie. Many years later, it was her granddaughter who was crowned as a Liberation princess for the Miss Guam Nisei Association. She was the young lady I chaperoned to Japan, which was her prize.

I find Tan Magdalena credible with this particular story as she was also close to Ms. Sasakura and a few other issei. She spoke English, having somehow spoken the language in her childhood. I never knew what school she attended and whether she graduated at all. But she spoke good English.

Around the beginning of July, Tåtan Kåcha and a group that included my grandfather and Tan Magdalena's father were summoned by the Japanese commander for a meeting at an undisclosed venue at the close of the war. All that was known was the location was up north. According to Tan Magdalena, the issei numbered a dozen, while others felt there were more than 20. Tåtan Kåcha was part of the group as its leader. The others remain nameless except for my Tåtan Dera' because the other families have yet to ascertain or acknowledge the mystery behind their disappearance.

It appeared that the men were summoned to discuss some aspect of the Japanese empire's role during the war — exoneration of would-be crimes, promises of prosperity if and when Japan was declared the victor in World War II, the sharing of material wealth to be given by the emperor in his dominion, and other glorious promises — all speculation floated among many of the issei. No one could substantiate further details as the war, the island's liberation, and its rebuilding took precedence over everything else. Everyone, both CHamoru and Nikkei, were just relieved that they'd be rescued and liberated by the United States.

The men, headed by Tåtan Kåcha, were herded into cramped quarters, again, this was shared by Tan Magdalena, who admitted to a sketchy recollection. She said two other individuals were with the men, Ms. Masumi Sasakura and, of course without a doubt, Tun Battasåt Nakasone. Also with them were three Japanese commanders whose names were not specified.

Because of Tun Battasåt's assertion that Ms. Sasakura was a mistress to one of the men, it was he who brought her to the attention of Japanese officials. She was brought in to witness what transpired to those issei. She was threatened that if she refused cooperation, she would be stripped of her business on Guam, sent back to Japan as a disgraced has-been geisha, and, as a further threat, she'd be penniless and roam the streets as a beggar. It was Tan Magdalena, who, at the close of the war, persisted in getting this confession from Ms. Sasakura. However, Ms. Sasakura, aside from witnessing the interrogation, punishment, and torture of the men, was frightened beyond measure. In her mental state, she blocked out the ordeal as, she said, there were no words to describe what she witnessed.

The only thing she remembered was that all the issei, whom she was forced to watch, were told to perform a suicide ritual of stabbing themselves in the deep gut of their body. She said she then blacked out and was carried out of the quarters before the actual self-stabbing happened. She said she woke up and found herself alone, mosquito-bitten, and wet from a heavy rainstorm. She remembered nothing else, not even her whereabouts, other than it was extremely dark and she was in some deep jungle in the dead of night. She didn't even see Tun Battasåt when she woke. She said she walked alone, cold, wet, puffy with mosquito bites, dirty, thirsty, and hungry. She found herself at the Plaza De España in Hagåtña, still in darkness.

Hence, the bodies of the men, including Tåtan Kåcha, were never found nor given proper burials. Ms. Sasakura, Tun Battasåt, and the three Japanese military commanders were the only people to have witnessed the interrogation, torture, and demise of those issei who disappeared.

Sadder still was that many of the Nikkei, who had no knowledge of the whereabouts of their patriarchs, devoted much of their lives trying to piece together what may possibly have happened. Rumors also spread like wildfire. Some speculated that the men were caught between the crossfires of the invading U.S. Marines and the Japanese; that they collaborated with the enemy by fighting against the United States; that they were secretly shipped off to Saipan or to Japan; or that they were buried alive if they didn't die from their self-stabs. Still, others claimed that the issei had joined the list of renegade Japanese stragglers who were military soldiers and refused to surrender at the close of the war. To this day, the fate of these issei remains a mystery.

CHAPTER 25

At War's End

JIRO'

Gossip and innuendo continued to run rampant. The locals started to have hope when word spread that the Americans were nearby in the Pacific, preparing to rescue the island from the foreign invaders. Many began doing daring deeds like hiding American flags. Some began speaking in broken English to the consternation of the Japanese commanders. The song "Uncle Sam" was sung at random, often within earshot of Japanese soldiers. There was hope anew. The residents of Malesso' retaliated against the Japanese soldiers in their village.

However, instead of hope and joyous expectations among the Nikkei, there was only deep-seated fear and uncertainty. Several issei and their wives began telling their children and adult sansei to prepare for death. Included among them were the families of Tan Engracia Morita, Tan Emilia Ozone, Tun Isidro Komatsu, and Tun Agusto Kiyuna. Even young children as young as age three were told by fearful mothers that they were soon to meet God in the afterlife, although the young children had no concept of God or the afterlife. Word reached Guam that many Japanese had committed suicide at Banzai Cliff in Saipan. Included among them were supposed Nikkei. People in Guam assumed that what happened in Saipan was, most likely, expected to happen in Guam among the Nikkei.

With Tåtan Dera's whereabouts still unknown, Nåna didn't waste any time talking to us. We were numb. The women in my clan could not stop crying. Nånan Dera' clutched rosary beads in her right hand as she spoke with a steady voice. I know she tried to remain calm as it appeared that the plight of the family was now in her hands. Although unsure of Tåtan Dera's status, she somehow managed to have faith and never once doubted he was still alive. As for us, children and adults, we couldn't tell if there was fear anymore, only the anticipation of pending death, for which, of course, no one in the family was prepared. To soothe our souls, Då and Auntie Måme' recited the rosary meant for those who died. I'm not sure if everyone felt relief or calm. I felt frozen, helpless, unsure of what to do. I was inclined to think that I would face my fate with God at my side. It was surreal.

With the dread of impending death, the Nikkei were beside themselves. Still, toward the close of the war, none of their CHamoru relatives bothered to seek them out to see if they needed help or even companionship during those last hours before the American bombardment.

The Japanese herded people to the concentration camp in Manenggon. Along the way, massacres were committed at CHagui'an, Asinan, Tå'i, Fenna, Mangilao, and other isolated places. It was in Malesso' where the residents there took their fate into their own hands and fought back, but not until many villagers were massacred at Tinta' and Fåha'. This rebellion also extended to Atatte, an area beyond the village boundary, an account that Tun Jose M. Torres wrote about in his book.

Everyone turned to the holy rosary. The news of the demise of Påle' Jesus Baza Dueñas and a companion had started to reach certain families and, as in all things with rumors, gossip, and innuendoes, people had a hard time understanding, much less, believing the truth about his torture and death. Those who were brought to the Manenggon camp began thinking that they, too, were going to be wiped off the face of the earth.

The Nikkei were not forced to march to Manenggon. However, they also didn't know what was going on. They stayed put. They didn't know about the U.S. Marines arrival or of the island's liberation, until the marines showed up at their hiding places, instructing them to go to Tutuhan or Hågat to the stockades.

Not knowing that the war had ended, especially among those families whose patriarchs mysteriously disappeared up north, they complied and made their way to Tutuhan. The Nikkei closest to Hågat were instructed to go to the Hågat stockade and were joined by others from Yo'ña, Ipan, Talo'fo'fo, Piti, Fenna, Inalåhan, and Humåtak. They were routed to Camp Bright at Gå'an Point.

CHAPTER 26

The Tutuhan and Hågat Stockades

JIRO'

The terms concentration camp, internment camp, and stockade designated three distinctions in the mindset of the local community.

U.S. concentration camps were created by an Executive Order by President Roosevelt. The order forcibly relocated and incarcerated at least 125,284 people of Japanese descent in the United States. These concentration camps were in California, Arizona, Wyoming, Colorado, Utah, and Arkansas, and were referred to as internment camps. These states were considered the western interior of the country. Executive Order 9066 was signed following the attack on Pearl Harbor.

On Guam, however, it was the Japanese forces under the command of General Takashina, the Japanese commander, who ordered the entire civilian population of Guam to move to Manenggon, as well as other established concentration camps. There were no specific numbers recorded, but thousands of people, from infants to the elderly, were forced to march the long, arduous trek through the southern interior of the island to a valley where a river ran alongside it. The river was considered a blessing as it was where people drank water, caught river fish and shrimp, and did their laundry and bathed.

Merriam-Webster's Dictionary and Thesaurus defines a stockade as an enclosure, enclosed by posts and stakes, for defense or confinement. This, most significantly, was what was familiar to the Nikkei. There was the Tutuhan (Agana Heights near what would eventually be the U.S. Naval Hospital) stockade, as well as Camp Bright in Hågat next to Gå'an Point's small U.S. Marines outpost.

The stockade was reportedly built by American soldiers to confine local people who were pro-Japanese. I don't remember seeing these pro-Japanese locals. It seemed that the stockade held only Nikkei families and their children, who had suffered through the war with me and the rest of the island community. Pale' Eric Forbes mentioned that Saipanese-CHamoru were confined there also. An elderly woman he spoke to who appeared on video described the people from Saipan who she said were there. I thought about the interpreters and the translators who were recruited by the Japanese military officials. Since I didn't know any of them, I'm assuming that they were the ones confined along with the Nikkei who were sent there. They were probably in another section of the stockade.

The stockade was quite large and divided into different sections that housed different groups, such as orphans, widows, widowers, elderly men or women, and others.

The area that the Nikkei families were assigned to consisted of Quonset huts. Each Quonset's standard size was 20 by 48 feet, and its top section reached a radius of 16 feet. About three to four families lived in one of four partitioned sections inside, and both sides had entrances that were also exits. It became a compromised agreement that the members of two families entered on one side, while the other two used the entrance on the other side. It was fortunate that screens covered both sides so that the breeze could waft in and out, making the quarters cool and comfortable. A kitchenette for each of the families was small enough and allowed for private cooking, although three meals a day were delivered to everyone from the military mess hall. The partitioned walls separating the families were built up to 10 feet only, leaving about 5 to 6 feet of space above the walls for the breeze to flow through. The only problem was that voices, sounds, movement, and clatter of any sort could be heard by all the families. The theft of money, personal items, and other important belongings did not happen as people trusted their neighbors. A helping hand between or among families was always rendered, even for the care and discipline of children.

Toilet and shower facilities were shared. They were located in another Quonset hut near the center of the compound. It was the same size as our living quarters, but privately partitioned and divided to accommodate males and females. It also had good drainage, ample paper products, and disposable trash bins on the outside of both ends where people disposed of trash from their living quarters. The facility was for everyone, but there was privacy in the toilets and the showers.

I remember keeping close to our living quarters because Nånan Dera' seemed to need me most of the time to fetch, clean, straighten our quarters, and help my mother and aunts, as we were housed in the same Quonset with three other families, many of whom had young children. Uncle John, as usual, was not with us most of the time as he was always off gallivanting goodness knows where. He only came to the stockade to eat, sleep, and leave again, usually at the crack of dawn. It wasn't long before he married Mercedes Acquiningoc and settled at her family property in Sinahånña. His early adult years were sketchy as I was under the guidance and care of Nåna and Tåtan Dera'. I was truly their right hand in daily affairs. The only aunt who wasn't confined with us at the stockade was Auntie Nena, who'd been under grandaunt Nan Låna's care. Auntie Nena was already married, too, while we were still at the stockade. I knew much later that she, along with the families of Nåna's siblings kept close to the Balitres of the Tomhom family clan. None of us ever knew if they'd been confined at the concentration camp in Manenggon. I realized, long after, that the immediate family had practically no knowledge of Auntie Nena's life during those war years. I don't know if she ever shared with her siblings and mother what went on in the household of Nan Låna' and the CHetton relatives in Tomhom.

Life was pleasant. We were provided meals, laundry supplies, and toiletries. We were free to come and go at all hours of the day or night. That, to me, was reason enough for Uncle John to come and go as he pleased.

Military officials used the term stockade to tell us that we had to be there.

It was also an internment camp, much like the concentration camps. It was here that I began to learn the English language as I began talking to the soldiers who patrolled our section. There were always three to five walking around, making sure that the Nikkei was comfortable and that no conflicts occurred.

Tun Takayoshi Okamitsu, baptized early on as a Catholic and named Jose, was summoned with his family to be confined at the Tutuhan stockade, just like us, at the close of the war. He was told it was an internment camp. He passed this information on to the rest of us. He said it was established by the U.S. President's executive order that decreed that people of Japanese descent, even those who were U.S. citizens — this applied to the mainland, not to us on Guam as the Organic Act did not become law until 1950 — were to be incarcerated in isolated camps for the duration of the war. However, the stockade didn't confine Nikkei families during the war. They confined us AFTER the war.

Unlike Guam, the Nikkei interned on the U.S. mainland camps were released in 1945, while those on Guam began their confinement not long after July 21, 1944. Unlike internment camps, everyone referred to the Tutuhan confinement as a stockade where it was supposed to be a prisoner-of-war camp for Japanese military soldiers. Tun Takayoshi Okamitsu and Tan Emilia Ozone said they never saw anyone whom they thought was a Japanese soldier. The people there were Nikkei families, as far as they knew. Even I thought the same. Because we were in one section, the other sections weren't accessible to us.

On a Superstock page of the *Sydney Morning Herald*, a photo of 2,600 Japanese troops, who were the garrison of the Rota surrender, was shown. The caption read that they were within the confines of the Prisoner of War Stockade on Guam on September 24, 1945. The stockade was located 50 miles south of Guam, at an American base. I assumed it must be at Camp Bright at Ga'an Point. I'd never gone there but communicated after the war with others who'd been confined there. I didn't know about the Rota group of stragglers. Camp Bright was close to the early U.S. Naval Station, which became a huge base after the war and housed military families who were assigned duty stations in Guam.

The U.S. Island Command established the Tutuhan Stockade as headquarters. The U.S. military conducted an intense search of Japanese stragglers, soldiers who hadn't yet surrendered.

In Hågat, the small number of Nikkei families confined there received a different kind of treatment separate from the families in Tutuhan. Although the locals also called the Hågat facility a stockade, it was referred to as a refugee camp. It was located near the Orote Peninsula.

Tun Jose said the officials who ran the stockade in Tutuhan had medical personnel take daily specimens of feces, urine, and blood from the Nikkei and their children. No explanation was ever given as to why that was necessary, and lab test results weren't ever disclosed to them. Tun Antonio Akiyama and Tan Emilia confirmed these facts, and both shared that every man, woman, and child was administered inoculations, four pockmarks on the upper part of the left arm.

In the '60s and the '70s, if someone saw the pockmarks, they were marked as being of Japanese descent and having been confined at the stockade in Tutuhan. It was said that while the specimens and inoculations occurred, not once did anyone ever have their hair checked for lice infestation. It must have been an oversight of the medical personnel. Stories of the Tutuhan stockade differed somewhat from the Hågat stockade, Tun Florencio Yoshida, who was confined with his family in Hågat, said no specimens were taken there, nor were they given inoculations.

Two sansei whom I talked to said they were confined in Hågat as youngsters with their families. They couldn't recall any medical specimens being taken. Much later, after thinking about my meeting with them, I regretted that I didn't ask to have them roll up their sleeves to see whether their forearms had the tell-tale pockmarks of inoculations. Tun Takayoshi Okamitsu, Tun Antonio Akiyama, and Tan Emilia Ozone, who were at the stockade in Tutuhan showed me theirs. My cousins and I have ours, and sometimes, we'd compete with one another to see whose pockmarks were bigger.

While the Nikkei families were confined to the stockade, the CHamoru who were liberated from Manenggon were granted a return to their villages to begin rebuilding their lives and their homes. The Nikkei weren't given this privilege.

Then there were the people who made it a point to go to the Tutuhan stockade daily — not because they were held there, but for another purpose. They'd stand along the road and the gate, jeering, mocking, and screaming obscenities at the Nikkei families. They threw garbage and dog feces and hurled gallons or bottles full of urine, human or otherwise. This happened at all hours of the day and night.

Hagåt, however, reported no hecklers at their gate. The people there were also allowed to come and go freely. The stockade in Hågat housed a sentry with uniformed guards. The sentry fronted Gå'an Point, which also housed a small military platoon. The Nikkei's confinement area was located a bit further from the entrance and the main road. The sentry guards didn't allow a gathering of any sort nor did they provide space to accommodate hecklers.

Although provided three meals a day, the Nikkei left Tutuhan in search of fresh fruits and vegetables, and other provisions from their ranches or from the scant few non-Nikkei relatives or friends who'd help them. Sometimes designated members of their household were seen bringing back bedding, pots, pans, dishes, utensils, household items, and sometimes prepared food. Others clutched religious statues and documents. One teenager carried her mother's wedding gown into the stockade.

The confined Nikkei in Tutuhan would return to the stockade and endure the hecklers and insults along the way. CHamoru children, encouraged by their elders, ran after Nikkei children, threw rocks, pulled their hair, spit at them, tore clothing, and tripped them. One group of teenagers ganged up on twin sisters who were punched, kicked, whipped with tree branches, and scratched on arms, legs, and faces until they bled.

What was sad was that many, if not most, of the hecklers were relatives, even siblings, of the women who married issei.

I witnessed this firsthand as I saw a Balitres aunt, husband, two daughters, and a son actually throw garbage at me and call me names. Their son goaded me into a fistfight. I made sure I gave him a bloody nose. My grand-mother sobbed and tried to stop the fight as she was cussed at by her cousin. Auntie Måme' and Då stopped the fight, and together, we walked Nåna back to our quarters. Daily or nightly, heartrending sobs could be heard in many of the scattered Quonset huts.

I witnessed much of the bullying and beatings. I'd grit my teeth when-ever I saw what was happening, especially toward young children and girls. I couldn't help but join in their defense when I saw such violence, especially as many of the Nikkei were my friends. The Nikkei boys fought back, and I let them without interference, but I was close by just in case. Sometimes, the heckling teenage boys would get much worse than what they bargained for because the Nikkei could truly pack a wallop. I was proud of them. I avoided these skirmishes because Nåna, my mother, and aunts urged me to ignore the heckling, hurry past the jeering crowd, make my way home to our quarters, and proceed to do the numerous chores that lay waiting for me.

My cousin Saburo accompanied many of the children. He was left alone by bullies because he had a reputation for being a fighter in the village and at school. When he fought, he made sure that the opponent ended up with a bloody nose and plenty of bruises that weren't something to brag about. It was unfortunate that he wasn't able to provide daily or hourly services as a body-guard, because, like me, Nåna also assigned him to leave the stockade for tasks. We never left together or did the same thing, but we would meet each other on the way back to the stockade, usually before dusk. His brother Shiro was like me. He also ignored the hecklers and concentrated on his work at our quarters.

Through the rumor mill, it was heard that a War Crimes Tribunal took place in a permanent building not far from the stockade. U.S. military officials, island leaders, and others were a part of the proceedings. I didn't know what was going on, much less, what happened there. I didn't even know if there was media coverage as our island still didn't have the possibility of news cameras or journalists. We didn't know the identities of those who were in attendance at the proceedings. We could tell they weren't local because they were blonde men or women, with freckles and wearing the latest American fashions or wearing military uniforms. I noticed just two or three African Americans who were obviously officers. They were in full uniform, however. No one among us was allowed in or near the entrance to that building.

Early in the morning, often at the crack of dawn, many Nikkei, men and women, left the stockade and made their way downtown to seek work. Many, like Tun Luis Takimia, Tun Manet Kaneshiro, Tun Isidro Komatsu, Tun Bonifacio Suchida, and Tan Ana Watanabe went together to apply for jobs as bus drivers, cooks, janitors, ticket takers, trinket sellers, lawn maintenance crew, cashiers, truck drivers, gardeners, and even for bank teller positions. Many would-be employers would glance at the application forms and see the Japanese surnames, then refuse to consider them for hiring. Many weren't even given an interview of any sort. It was discouraging and disheartening. Some administrators of these offices even made derogatory remarks to the applicants.

This went on for months. There was no money to be had by the Nikkei. Business owners who were once a part of the commercial district in Hagåtña joined the throngs of unemployed, destitute, and penniless Nikkei. Their former property in the capital was deemed not theirs any longer, by whom, no one was certain. Other properties that included vehicles, merchandise from their shops, equipment and machinery, and household and business furnishings that weren't damaged from the bombardment weren't returned or compensated for. The matter wasn't an open issue, either for discussion or settlement, and the issue died without any form of acknowledgment or accountability.

It was then that some families decided to change their surnames. Soon, hirings started to happen as applications began seeing surnames like Blas, Santos, Cruz, Torres, and Guerrero, despite the fact that the applicants had the telltale light complexion, slanted eyes, and even exaggerated English. The Nikkei took great pains to practice English among themselves to appear as if schooled in the ways of the American language. They tried to be fancy.

The refugee camp in Hågat ended in 1946 and the Tutuhan stockade closed in 1949. Before they closed, command officials assigned Nikkei families, five at a time, to designated villages. No one was allowed to return to their previous village, which was largely Hagåtña. They had to obey the new instructions. Many village commissioners initially had a say in these assignments, but they had to accept the final decisions of military stockade officers.

I remember standing in the midst of these assignments, as Nånan Dera', my mother, and Auntie Måme' asked me to be with other Nikkei as these announcements were made. My knowledge and use of the English language were progressing well. The U.S. military soldiers I'd befriended allowed me to stand with the adults when I explained that I needed to translate for them. I saw Tan Magdalena Matsuyama, or Mag, who was my courier companion during the war. Because she spoke English and was at ease translating from English to CHamoru, she stood next to the commander, translating verbatim to the rest of the crowd of mostly Nikkei elders.

Although some Nikkei families, in groups of five, had already left the Tutuhan stockade for the villages assigned to them, there were still Nikkei families confined and waiting for a village assignment. Families like Tan Emilia's didn't get assigned until most everyone had been sent off to their respective villages. I think they were the last of the families to leave.

Of the 12 identified villages, the surnames of the following comprised the assignments:

1. AGANA HEIGHTS:	Fujikawa, Haniu, Miyasaki, Sakakibara, Suzuki
2. AGAT:	Asanoma, Ishizaki, Sonoda, Tayama, Yamashita
3. ASAN:	Gokita, Ige, Kitamura, Yamaguchi, Yamamoto
4. BARRIGADA:	Hamamoto, Ochiai, Okazaki, Shimoda, Yokoi
5. DEDEDO:	Akiyama, Murakami, Okada, Sawada, Shimizu
6. PITI:	Hatoba, Maiyami, Miyashita, Muroi, Yamanaka
7. SANTA RITA:	Ito, Noda, Sugiyama, Tajima, Yoshida
8. SINAJANA:	Hara, Imaizumi, Iwatsu, Onodera, Ooka
9. TALOFOFO:	Guioko, Ikeda, Matsunaga, Sakamoto, Sugiyama
10. TAMUNING:	Bukikosa, Dejima, Kanesi, Shinohara, Tanaka

11. YIGO: Ogawa, Kochi, Matsumiya,
                           (perhaps Machimia), Takano
12.YONA: Asano, Ichihara, Okiyama, Sayama, Sudo

Many villages became a part of the municipalities of the current and
modern geography. Sumai was no more as it was destroyed by the invading air
strikes of Japan. CHålan Pågu, Humåtak, Ma'ina, Otdot, Inalåhan, Maite', Mangilao, Mongmong, Piti, and To'to were largely small settlements and ranchlands. Malesso', too, was a small village, and it wasn't assigned Nikkei, perhaps
because of the massacres at Tinta' and Fåha'. There weren't additional written
information on where other families were assigned to, but to be sure, Nikkei
families were not assigned to the capital city of Hagåtña. These assignments
continued throughout that year and the next. It extended to the final year
when the stockade at Tutuhan officially closed in 1949 as verified by Tan Emilia
Ozone. She didn't disclose where she and her family were assigned.

The following surnames weren't assigned a village, but they did appear
in the 1920 census, and in subsequent birth, marriage, and death announcement records: Sukoko, Suyona, Takimia, Yamasaki, Fuhikawa, Iseyaki, Suchida,
Yamashiro, Inouye, Kaneshiro, Oseda, Higuchi, Hattori, Suyona, Miamoto,
Sosoko, Ozawa, Tachibana, Tareyama, and Wada. There's no record of where
these Nikkei were assigned after the close of the Tutuhan or Hågat stockades.

Unlike the CHamoru who rebuilt homesteads on original properties in
the villages, many Nikkei lived temporarily in makeshift dwellings amid unwel-
coming hostile neighbors. Distrust and avoidance of local wives by relatives,
siblings, and former friends in their newly assigned places continued. As if in
a third-world country, issei husbands, nisei children, and sansei grandchildren
were discriminated against almost daily. Nikkei families, as before, commiserated among themselves. If help was needed, the pre-teen couriers among
their children continued to serve as a communication network. That was the
only relief that the Nikkei families had in post-war Guam.

Through intermarriage, land inheritance because of wives, economic
opportunities, and other societal factors, movement to assigned villages even-

tually became permanent after a few more years. Many of the surnames in some of the villages have retained their domicile and succeeding generations of families continue to live there.

Some experiences were considered mild to some Nikkei, who chose to live out their lives in Guam by exhibiting patience, endurance, and a commitment to withstand whatever came their way. Others, whose experiences were to extremes, including rapes, torture and beheadings, near-fatal punishment, and unexplained disappearances, grouped their families together and waged a savings scheme for the purchase of airline tickets to leave Guam. Many urged sons to enlist in the U.S. Navy post-Organic Act. When President John F. Kennedy established the island as an open travel zone, droves of families, many Nikkei, scrimped and saved hard-earned money, sold material possessions such as land and personal property, and moved to the U.S. mainland leaving Guam for good.

CHAPTER 27

Search for Tåtan Dera'

JIRO'

Our family, as well as other Nikkei, spent several weeks that stretched into months, and finally years of confinement at the Tutuhan Stockade. War was already over and many of us saw the rebuilding of the island in the various villages as we were allowed to go to and from the stockade. The hecklers continued their daily routine, and we just ignored them. I, for one, would pass through them without a glance. Other Nikkei did the same, and the hecklers soon became a blur.

Aside from the daily taking of specimens from our bodies, inoculations, and three meals a day, we showered, did our laundry, and left the stockade for places that once were our homes, ranchlands, and former hideouts during the war—schoolyards, churches, and places like the bank and government offices. The U.S. military was kind to us, but they didn't speak to us either, except those soldiers who taught me English.

One elderly nisei woman took it upon herself to conduct two daily rosaries: the first one at the wee hours of the morning, as many men and women had the habit of reciting the rosary before the rest of the households began waking up, and the second one at 3 p.m., or thereabouts, for it was the Divine Mercy Chaplet.

Because school wasn't re-established or opened yet, a former teacher, a young local woman who married a nisei and chose to stay with him and his family at the stockade, began teaching many of the children who were willing to learn. She devised her own lessons, and soon, the children were engaged in spelling bees, arithmetic lessons, simple science, reading, history, singing, and artwork. She was innovative. Even teenagers became engaged by being aides and learning, too, at the same time. This kept the children occupied and away from the nearby hecklers.

One morning Nånan Dera' woke me up. She'd just finished reciting the rosary with other adults and had already prepared breakfast. What I remembered most of her in those days was always the hope in her voice that *"måtto tåtte siempre si Tåtan Dera',"* Tåtan Dera' would somehow return. He'd left at the height of the liberation, or maybe even at the moment the U.S. military soldiers landed at Assan or Hågat. It was in the stockade that she learned of the other Issei patriarchs who were also missing just like Tåta.

"Jiro', kahulo' i lahi-hu. Sigi ya un espiha fan si Tåta sa' siña ha' ti siña mamok- kat patsino tåya' ma'udai-ña para mågi. Espiha gi amånu na lugåt annai gaige gui' mohon!" (Jiro', wake up my son. Go and look for your grandpa because maybe he can't walk or maybe he doesn't have a ride to get here. Look for him at any place possible where he might be.)

I got up, washed my face, brushed my teeth, and ate a hurried breakfast. By this time, in late 1945, I was already 15 years old and was able to walk long distances. I left the stockade that morning.

It was a long walk down to Hagåtña, and while there, I learned that a bus was now available that could take people to places like Tamuneng, Dededu, Yigu, over to Mangilao, and back down to Hagåtña. Another bus took passengers to Assan, all the way to Hågat and back. I had never seen a bus before, much less rode in one, and it was free. There were long lines of people all the time. Sometimes the driver would allow people to stand in the bus aisles. Some drivers didn't allow it at all.

It was on this bus ride that I saw with my own eyes many places that had no vegetation, buildings, or development of any sort. The war had flattened many areas. There were makeshift lean-tos and crude huts. I saw a parachute hoisted on some long poles that served as a shelter for a family or families.

There were also people, young and old, who walked the distance along the side of the road to get from one place to another. It was in Mangilao when a short man boarded the bus. With his first look at me, because of my slanted eyes, he knew right away that I was a nisei or, should I say, sansei.

He demanded that I stand in the middle of the bus where every rider could see me in full view as he obviously wanted to subject me to shame. He began talking loudly, scolding me first, then his voice pitched to screaming and cussing at the same time. He told me about my people. and how shameful we all were during the most tragic time in the history of the island. All Japanese *mestisu* (half-caste), as he said it, should be killed en masse or burned at the stake. All eyes looked at me, and he let me have it full blast. If he could have whipped me to shreds, he probably would have. I took all his insults as it came spilling from his mouth. Without a word, I just stood, kept my mouth shut, and my eyes glued to the floor of the bus, not knowing whether to talk back, cuss in return, or make faces at him. All that flashed through my mind was how I'd remember Nånan Dera', Auntie Måme', my mother and Då repeatedly say, "render respect to elders and keep quiet unless spoken to." But this man was certainly not talking to me. He was screaming at me, behaving without an inkling of respect toward me. I inwardly seethed with anger.

The next stop was back at the capital city. I was the first to get off the bus, and the man continued to scream his head off. I waited to see if the passengers gave him a round of applause or even a standing ovation, but nothing happened. I just breathed a sigh of relief. That was the only time I ever rode a bus in my life, and I never did again.

I never forgot that man. Years later he ran for public office. I never told my grandmother or the elders about what he did to me during that bus ride. When he ran for public office, I joined the opposing political party that fielded an opponent. I voted constantly and continually against this man for whom I had no respect. When I began my business, I donated to his opponents' campaigns as he was obviously popular and continued winning his seat. He may have served several years, but he was nothing to me. From that moment on, I was the first of my family to join an opposing political party, which relatives speculated and talked about out of my earshot, but it was this man who steered me to the opposing party all the way into my late adult years. Throughout the rest of my life, without any explanation, I instructed all my children and grandchildren to follow the political party that I chose.

I awoke every morning at an ungodly hour to walk long distances to avoid riding the bus. I did all the tasks expected of me, and often, I'd leave still in darkness before sunrise. Nånan Dera wanted me to avoid the gathered hecklers. They numbered in the dozens. On rainy days, only a few individuals and small families showed up, gathered, and performed their routine of humiliation, obscenities, and insults. As I said earlier, I ignored them all.

I walked for miles to many places. I'd retrace my steps and venture off into different areas despite my previous day or week's visit to the same area. These searches went on for a long time. It stretched into weeks and months. It was on my birthday that I realized I'd searched for Tåtan Dera' for more than a year. I scoured over the northern terrain and went as far as the beaches along the northernmost coast. I'd walked into deep jungles despite my fear of the supernatural and the ancient spirits. I avoided ranches and homes of families just so that I wouldn't have to explain myself. I'd turn around and head for the nearest exit if I entered private property. I entered caves and felt my way in the darkness. I crawled into pillboxes that had been bombed and nearly destroyed. I entered abandoned homes damaged or destroyed in the aftermath of the bombardment. My biggest fear was running into people whose sentiments were the same as the man on the bus. I didn't want to be subjected to insults and perhaps being manhandled by an individual or a group, including families. My stamina was truly tested as I'd walked for hours without a drink of water or a bite to eat. I'd often come across fruit-laden trees like mangoes, papayas, sweet sop, and custard apple, but I'd steer clear away, oftentimes, as they grew in ranchlands. An irate rancher was another person high on my list to avoid.

I went to Tomhom. I'd see elder relatives, render my respect, and sometimes, just take a nibble of something offered. I drank water until I was full. Then, I'd continue. From there, I'd revisit our old home in Tokcha', which was now abandoned and destroyed, overgrown with weeds, bushes, and coconut trees. There was nothing else there.

I walked to southern Guam and hiked through the boonies, up the mountains, down the hills, alongside streams and rivers, remote areas fronting the calm sea. Once I came across a decayed body abandoned and perhaps missed by cleanup crews. It was on the coast somewhere between Humåtak and Hågat. I ran away really fast. In places like Inalåhan, Malesso', and Sånta Rita, there were houses where I just crossed quietly in shady areas and continued into the jungle. Sumai, too, was abandoned. The ruins of the bombing that started the island's path to World War II, and many abandoned and vacant homes, buildings, and landmarks were left to the elements. I paid my respects at the cemetery because I remembered that relatives of my great-grandmother, Nånan Leonora de Bae Santos, were buried there. I then continued in the jungles past Åpla', Tepungan, Piti, and Assan.

I'd end up in Hagåtña where our former home was. The area where the house and store stood was completely flattened. Other familiar places were no longer recognizable such as the church. Parts of the Plaza de España and the Sirena Bridge were still intact.

Then, I'd walk up Okso' San Ramon, veer right to Tutuhan, and head straight to the stockade. I'd tell Nånan Dera' the same sad news: I had no luck again with the whereabouts of Tåtan Dera'. She'd just cross herself, hug me, and then lead me to the dining table for a nourishing meal that she cooked especially for me.

Those moments left me sad. I'd wished that, instead, Nåna opened the door of our quarters and saw me with my Tåta as he stood next to me or as I carried him as he was exhausted, injured, or sick. I'd play those scenes in my mind so often that I'd often dream that I finally found Tåtan Dera'. Unfortunately, I never did.

PART FOUR

CHAPTER 28

Sansei

PETER

I'm a sansei. I learned that at age six. I learned on a day when I had played war with other kids. Our game wasn't cowboys versus Indians, but Americans against Japanese.

We'd shoot at the make-belief enemy, while under houses, crouched behind outhouses, abandoned refrigerators and freezers, parked cars, next to *bateha siha* (outside flat wooden sinks with suspended faucets), various yard structures, and bushes of hibiscus, plumeria, candlebush, parsma berry, ginger, orchids, and climbable trees.

It was all fun. Afterward, my pals and I would each count our cents, which included a lot of pennies, go to Baza's Store behind my house, buy Bireley's Cream Soda, Coca-Cola, Juicy Fruit gum, pixy sticks, and our favorite candy, the Big Hunk. Then, we'd walk to someone's front yard, sit under the trees, eat, drink, and exchange friendly banter. It was all so innocent.

Oftentimes, we'd sing, off-key and boisterous. The lyrics went like this:

> Manmanggåna i Amerikånu, Manma pedde i CHapanes.
> (The Americans have won, the Japanese have lost)
> We have fought our country's battles, in the air, on
> land, and seas...

Of course, the song had no ending, or, at least, I don't remember the ending, but it was a bonding song for the neighborhood boys who had engaged in make-believe combat. There was another favorite song we sang, but with our own lyrics. It was a song made famous by the late and honorable Tun Pete Siboyas. I later learned that Siboyas wasn't his last name, but his a.k.a. name. He was Tun Pete Rosario who I was fortunate to know toward the last years of his life. His song was a classic in Tan Carmen Santos' production of *Guam's History in Songs*:

> Oh, Uncle Sam, Sam, my dear Uncle Sam, won't you please come back to Guam?

> Ilek-ña i CHapanes na siha number one, ilek-ña i Amerikånu bai lachai hao bumomb.
> (*The Japanese said that they're number one, the Americans said that they all will be bombed*)

> Oh, Uncle Sam, Sam, my dear Uncle Sam, won't you please come back to Guam.

> Ilek-ña i CHapanes na siha number two, Ilek-ña i Amerikånu na un lakes hao di'åpblo.
> (*The Japanese said that they're number two, the Americans said the heck with all of you*)

> Oh, Uncle Sam, Sam, my dear Uncle Sam, won't you please come back to Guam.

> Ilek-ña i CHapanes na siha number three, Ilek-ña i Amer-ikånu, hu cho'me hao ni' takure.
> (*The Japanese said that they're number three, the Americans said they'll spill a kettle of hot water on them*)

Oh, Uncle Sam, Sam, my dear Uncle Sam, won't you please
come back to Guam.

The song was a favorite of ours because it contained the numbers up to
10, and each one of us had the task of finding a rhyming CHamoru word to the
English number before it broke into the plea for Uncle Sam to return to us.
It was never the same lyrics. It varied from boy to boy, day by day, and after
make-believe battle after make-believe battle. We'd often laugh ourselves silly
until our mothers summoned us home, yelling from across neighbors' yards.
It was often near dusk when we'd part.

It was after one of these adventures that my mother sat me down and
talked to me about the war years for the first time.

She shared her experiences and stories about her siblings, relatives near
and far, and the mysterious disappearance of my grandfather Zenpei Jito.

I began piecing two and two together.

Once, as a youngster, I sold a case or two of empty Coca-Cola bottles at
the bottling plant located on the other side of the village highway. I was short-
changed by nearly a half-dollar, while my companions Percy and Wilfred both
had their full share of $1.20 each, compared to my 70 cents.

We brought in empty bottles of Coca-Cola that we collected from under
houses, bushes, trash bins, junk yards, and out-of-the-way places. We stacked
the bottles in wooden cases that we'd finagle from the mom-and-pop stores
with a promise to return them when done. My friends and I would walk for
several blocks, lugging the cases of bottles on our wheeled hand-made carts to
the bottling company. Each bottle was worth a nickel, paid by the saleslady at
the company counter. The money was a fortune for children like me, as it took
weeks, maybe months, to accumulate enough bottles to make the effort worthwhile. Many enterprising kids, like us, looked forward to the bottle hunts,
but carrying them on the makeshift carts, even with wheels, was heavy work.
It required crossing the major roadway that ran from Hagåtña up the hill of
Sinahånña and into Otdot, CHålan Pågu, then Mangilao or Yo'ña.

My companions and I found the effort worthwhile. With our money, we'd either splurge on snacks at the neighborhood store or even at Butler's Store, which was next door to the bottling company. The saleslady who tended to us at the Coca-Cola Company knew Percy, Wilfred, and me by name. She never addressed me by name, only with the moniker Jap. I didn't realize it was a term referring to my lineage, and not in a nice way. She'd always try to swindle me with half of my earnings, and I'd protest with the help of my friends. We'd accumulated the same number of empty bottles to sell. I didn't know that the saleslady was someone who was related to my mother and had stood outside the stockade in Tutuhan, hurling insults at my family when they were confined there.

I learned who she was when my mother accompanied me to the Bottling Company one day because the saleslady had refused to give me the full amount of money for my bottles. Percy had accompanied us as he was my witness. When my mother insisted on speaking to Mr. Butler, the company owner and general manager, regarding the saleslady's attitude, she relented and gave me the full amount I was owed. It was my mother who then told Percy and me that the saleslady was from a clan with whom she was related, and that the saleslady and her family were hecklers at the Tutuhan Stockade.

On another occasion, I was with my mother, who was a diabetic, at a clinic for a doctor's appointment. The local female receptionist ignored my mother completely and didn't attend to her. My poor mother waited quietly and patiently for nearly an hour until a blonde state-sider, who was the nurse, took notice of her and proceeded with her appointment. Although my mother never said anything, I saw the tears in her eyes, and I saw the look of hatred in that receptionist's eyes. They knew each other. The receptionist was one of the folks who stood outside the Tutuhan Stockade heckling the confined Nikkei. My mother told me much later that she was related to the receptionist, too. The receptionist, along with her immediate family, disowned my mother and her family because of the war. Instances like that became embedded in my mind.

One summer, I rode on a Liberation Day Parade float during the annual celebration. My family was a member of the Guam Nisei Association, and the group had been working on the final touches to their float, built in the park-ing lot of Fukuda Enterprises in Hagåtña. Before the parade, in early June, the crowning of a Miss Guam Nisei Association had taken place at the Hong Kong Gardens in Tamuning. As her prize, she was scheduled to go to Japan for a nine-day trip visiting historical and cultural sites, and to partake in an interview at the NHK Broadcasting station in downtown Tokyo. In an earlier chapter, I wrote about how my first cousin Jiro' had escorted the queen on that goodwill tour.

That parade was to be my very first ride on a parade float. Years before then, I'd watched with envy the parade participants and float riders along Marine Drive. For this parade, I was extremely excited as I was also going to wear some ancient Japanese warrior's attire that included a helmet, care-fully made by a member of the club. It wasn't a military soldier's helmet but an ancient Samurai warrior. The other children with me, who were slated to ride the float, too, had costumes carefully sewn by doting mothers and aunts. The costumes ranged from kimonos to parasols, period costumes of Japanese characters, and some were also legendary figures and gods and goddesses.

The float, too, involved much preparation that included boonie stomping for foliage, mosses, vines, trees and shrubs, gathering flowers, and miscella-neous vegetation. Late afternoons and into the night, the menfolk measured, cut lumber, sawed, hammered, and painted. The work involved many dozens of people, family members, men, women, teenagers, and even children.

On the day of the parade, I woke up early, showered, and changed into my costume. In the car, the driver carefully drove to where the float was parked on the parade route. I'm not sure who the other riders were on that float, but we were young, and we were all sansei, including the queen, who was the honored beauty atop the float. I don't recall adults riding on the float, just children, teenagers, and the queen.

As the parade inched along Marine Drive, floats and marching units before us all received applause. Well-wishers screamed their delight at the people either marching or riding, as, I'm sure, many were perhaps friends, relatives, or acquaintances. Not us. The crowd grew silent as our float passed.

No cheers, no clicking cameras, no applause greeted us. Some people diverted their attention to look elsewhere, talking and whispering to one another, and even eating, but it was deathly silent as our float made its way to the end. Some people gave us the middle finger. The grandstand was where we received a lukewarm reception. Some smiled and waved, but not the standing ovations received by the floats before us and the ones after. I remembered glancing over at our queen. She had tears running down her face. It slightly smeared her make-up, but she continued smiling as she waved at the unresponsive crowd.

After passing the grandstand, a man yelled an obscenity at us. Others joined in. Someone threw something at our float but it landed on the floor away from the children. In addition to the cussing, we were shown many more middle fingers, thumbs down, and mouthed words of "boo." Many of us children were bewildered by the unfriendliness and nasty reception.

Gone was the feeling of excitement, only fear. It was my first real lesson of how people still carried resentment toward Nikkei descendants. Mind you, the war ended way before I was born but the resentment and hatred persisted. I saw and felt it. This was 1960.

I went to public school all my life. From elementary through high school, I remember classmates with surnames of Imaizumi, Sudo, Okada, Takano, Ichihara, Murakami, Okazaki, Hamamoto, Imamura, Yokoi, Waki, Hara, Kanesi, Yamashita, Asano, and Iwatsu. In conversations, many of them shared experiences of indignities, especially name-calling.

It was during a conversation with Joe Imaye, whom I met in Honolulu, where he told me that he and his family moved to Idaho just before the signing of the Organic Act. His elders, still children at the time, witnessed the torture of a nisei uncle who was given a grenade, whose pin had been pulled, to hold. It exploded in his hands. The uncle's sin was the innocent, forgotten act of not bowing to a high-ranking commander whom he didn't know.

I met Clementina Aoki, who ended up living in Millington, Tennessee, at an AARP conference in Arizona. Clementina recalled how her mother and her family had to eat tadpoles and geckos as they'd been denied assistance of food and water by relatives who lived in one of the central villages. Her mother was married to an issei. The entire family moved to the States once they could afford to leave the island. Her elders considered it taboo to return to Guam for even a short visit.

Many others moved to the States the first chance they could. Several families with issei surnames are no longer a part of the fabric of island life. They wanted nothing more to do with Guam.

As I grew up, I learned other things along the way. I remembered rousing my mother from a delirious sleep where she was screaming, crying, and tossing about. The pillow wet with her tears. I pinched her nostril to stop her breathing momentarily to wake her as I had a hard time rousing her. I shook her body as I tried one thing after another. She had gasped for air, sitting up quickly, and was ready to hit me until she realized it was me. I asked her what she was dreaming about. She said she had watched as a man was beheaded by a soldier. She uttered the name, but I had no idea who he was. It was before my time. There were other times when I was able to rouse her from sleep. But the first time was further proof she had experienced her own horrors. After that, she refused to talk about the war years. I had to learn from others, and if my mother refused, so did her sisters. I didn't bother them. Once, I was tempted to talk to my Uncle John, but my brother Shiro' told me to let sleeping dogs lie.

I remembered being called names while growing up. The name-calling included affixations of Japanese-made products such as Kikkoman, nori, and miso. Once, a brother-in-law addressed my son and me as a "wangao," his own play on a word that designated our Asian features and he, by habit, mocked people who looked Asian. I compared his adjective with classmates who were also sansei. We had similar experiences that may seem funny but were what we considered insulting.

Life as a sansei was not a great thing for me. All I did was seek more information, which led me to my project of interviews in conjunction with my UOG class. My discoveries doing that project opened my eyes.

Much later, when I met and spoke to a local woman who was forced to be a comfort woman, I learned that there was another side to the island's claim for liberation, that Nikkei families didn't experience a joyous liberation.

In Antonio M. Palomo's book, *An Island in Agony*, the women were called Monday ladies as it was said that they provided sexual services to soldiers. Mondays were the days soldiers would report to a medical dispensary to be tested and given penicillin shots for gonorrhea or syphilis. Much later, too, CHamoru women were forced into sexual slavery and were snatched from their households, some as young as 14 years old. In the meantime, Korean women were brought in, and they, too, were forced to serve as comfort women. In and around the capital city where the soldiers were headquartered, scattered homes were designated as comfort homes. In my later career working for the Muscular Dystrophy Association, I met an elderly CHamoru who was married to a statesider. She shared that her home in Anigua was designated a comfort home for battalions of Japanese soldiers. She showed me her home back in 1976. The home that stood there is no longer there. A commercial three-story building stands in its place. It was, and still is, right along Marine Corps Drive.

The Nikkei had personal struggles, and experienced fear and mistreatment. As Tun Isidro Komatsu said, they were people, indeed, without a country. They had nowhere to go, no one to speak to, no one to share with, and no one to relate to as family or friends; they only had enemies. The mistrust, the betrayal, the turncoats, the haters, the bullies, the cruelty, and the thefts were all very real.

CHAPTER 29

The 1920 Census
PETER

It wasn't clear who conducted the 1920 Census of the Catholic Church. It also wasn't clear whether the information gathered for the census included information from what was then established as the parish churches from the different villages. The historic churches in Humåtak, Malesso', Inalåhan, Sumai, and Hagåtña, were, I believe, the only churches that existed in the early century and pre-war Guam. I know that the other village parishes came with the resettling of villages after the war. I remember wooden structures in Barigåda, Yo'ña, Tamuning, Dededu, Hågat, and my home village of Sinahånña. In addition, these were the churches where Bishop Apolinaris Baumgartner welcomed and assigned religious sisters to reside as they arrived from the United States. The nuns established and built convents, and eventually Catholic Schools. But, those were post-war ventures. When Typhoon Karen came and destroyed the island, construction of concrete structures sprung up in those villages.

Nevertheless, I found it difficult to ascertain the accuracy of the 1920 Census, and I fear it may be more inconclusive regarding the island's population count. The results were not publicized or made available to the public until sometime in the late '30s.

I found it convenient, though, that surnames of issei were indicated with the italicized word, Japones, and it became quite notable for later scrutiny and those seeking information about patriarchs who married into CHamoru families. Of note, was that surnames of other ethnicities, some of which were well known, included Wusstig, Scharff, Sgambelluri, Chaco, Gutierrez, as well as state-siders who also married CHamoru women like Elliott, McDonald, Portusach, Anderson, Butler, and Johnston were devoid of an ethnic reference. Somehow, only those with Japanese surnames were given the italicized indication of their origins. There were no italics for Italians, Germans, Filipinos, Americans, and others.

In my research, I searched specifically for the counts regarding the issei and, eventually, their families. The distinction of the italics proved helpful, but there were instances of the same names appearing again in another village. As an example, my grandfather Zenpei Jito was included in the village count of Hågat, which I found quite strange as, according to family accounts, he never lived anywhere near that village; rather, he resided originally in Tokcha' as a contract hire for Tåtan Kåcha, then Tomhom when he married my grandmother, then Hagåtña when he started a business, and back to Tokcha' as his place of refuge with his family for the duration of the war. Unfortunately, his untimely disappearance did not allow him time at the stockade or the move to Sinahånña for resettlement. He was, however, baptized at the Hagåtña church moments before he wed Nåna, and Nåna's family witnessed his baptism and his marriage to her.

Further, my great-grandmother, Nånan Leonora de Bae Santos, as per family accounts, was born in Sumai and grew up there, but she wasn't included in the 1920 Census. She was the eldest, but her succeeding nine siblings were included and counted. I don't know if this was an oversight or if maybe the recording of baptisms wasn't done at the time she was born.

Other surnames that did not appear in the census, appeared in birth, death, and marriage announcements in news columns of the *Guam Newsletter* and continued in the *Guam Recorder* before and after the census. This went to prove that the census was incomplete, and there was speculation that maybe only certain churches recorded baptisms, or that babies, due to hardship were never baptized, or that baptism took place maybe years later, and/or that babies born may have died not long after, as undisclosed or undiagnosed diseases like smallpox, influenza, malaria, etc. were isolated community epidemics. Unfortunately, the mimeographed records I found at the Micronesian Area Research Center (MARC) at the University of Guam did not disclose any information as to where the baptisms took place, whether at Humåtak, Malesso', Inalåhan, Sumai, and Hagåtña. I'm assuming that perhaps it was Hagåtña church where the 1920 Census was conducted, but I have no proof.

Below are the list of names that I found from the records at MARC, and I noted them down just based on the italicized distinction that was given:

Akiyama	Iseyaki	Muroi	Sudo
Asano	Isezaki	Noda	Sugiyama*
Asanoma	Ishizaki	Ochiai	Suyona
Bukikosa	Ito	Ogawa	Suzuki
Dejima	Iwatsu	Okada	Tajima
Fuhikawa	Jota*	Okazaki	Takamiya
Fujikawa	Kamo	Okiyama	Takano
Fukuda*	Kanagawa	Ono	Takatsu
Gokita	Kanesi	Onodera	Tanaka
Gokita*	Kitagawa*	Ooka	Tareyama*
Guioko	Kitamura	Oseda	Tayama
Hamamoto	Kobayashi	Ozone	Yamaguchi
Haniu	Kochi	Sakakibara	Yamamoto
Hara	Kokoro	Sakamoto	Yamanaka
Hatoba	Kurokawa	Sawada	Yamasaki*
Hatoba*	Kusunoki*	Sayama	Yamashita
Hattori	Machimia	Shibati	Yanada
Hirano	Maiyami	Shimizu	Yokoi
Hirayama	Matsunaga	Shimoda	Yoshida
Ichihara	Miamoto	Shinohara	
Ige	Miyasaki	Sokoko	
Ikeda	Miyashita	Sokoro*	
Imaizumi	Morita	Sosoko	
Inouye	Murakami	Suchida*	

It must be argued that the 1920 Census showed no specifics as to where issei and their families stayed, and whether there was permanence to their domicile. Apparently, the church had conducted its own census, in which births, marriages, and deaths were recorded, and there were no restrictions as to parish affiliation. In other words, a family, CHamoru or Nikkei, may live in Piti but choose to have sacraments in another parish church where perhaps the mother was from, as matriarchal adherence could have been taken into account. These situations occurred often, even municipalities could have conflicting information regarding where families were living. A family living in one village may have wanted to be affiliated with the village where they originally were from. Another challenge was perhaps a plantation contract worker may have been counted in the census, but the following year could have decided not to renew his contract and returned home to Japan. Essentially, his count as a resident of Guam became permanent unbeknownst to church officials. Some of the names listed were found in subsequent counts to this day.

As a final note, the names above with the asterisks (*) are names that weren't on the census, but around that time, as I mentioned, these surnames appeared in the *Guam Newsletter* or *The Guam Recorder* where family members who had been baptized, married, or died were listed. Together with the ones that were on the 1920 Catholic Church Census, they comprised the likely community of the Nikkei from the period of the 1900s to the 1940s just before World War II arrived on Guam. I didn't find any other census from the other Christian denominations like the Protestant mission that was also established on the island.

What was problematic for me, which I consider significant, was the tremendous misspellings of first and surnames. I must note that in 1920, the United States administration of the island through Naval governors was still new. Guam was still fresh off the influence of Spain with its language, religion, and traditions. CHamoru was a language devoid of an established written form until the 1960s and 1970s. English, mandated as the newly established education standard of the native CHamoru, was also in its infancy in 1920.

Therefore, spelling was not a primary lesson. The English alphabet, which was still a phenomenon, was now used in all written documentation on Guam. At that time, most writings were formulated by English-speaking individuals and not necessarily anyone from the CHamoru community.

Therefore, many names, first and last, were grossly misspelled in many documents about the native population, especially in birth, marriage, and death documents. For example, I've found variations of the spelling of my surname as it underwent an adaptation using the vowels in the English language. I've found my surname of ONEDERA written in many variations documented in handwritten letters, invitations, anecdotes, and even in passing with the introduction of the typewriter. My last name has appeared as Anadera, Anedara, Enedera, Enuadere, Inodera, Inuderra, Onydera, and Uniedera. My surname should be ONODERA but, according to a popular oral account, my grandmother, who relayed the information about herself on a government information sheet, had the listener/writer indicate her name the way she pronounced it. And, to this day, my surname has appeared in documented records as ONEDERA, misspelled as it is from the Japanese original ONODERA.

I use my surname as an example for I have noticed that some researchers make note of this, and while I don't dare include names from CHamoru or other ethnicities, the misspellings occurs often. To correct it would be costly to pursue legally. To me, the misspelling of names when indicated in vital statistics, surveys, ethnic records, etc., often contributed to inaccuracy and confusion.

CHAPTER 30

Nikkei Membership

PETER

In the '90s and into the new millennium, I was a member of the Guam Nikkei Association. The group met at the Sizzler's Restaurant in Hagåtña. It was an interesting group, a mix of noted personalities from the island and a few prosperous businessmen and civic leaders. There were a couple of men who came over from Saipan and attended meetings. I believe one was Absalon Waki, if I remember correctly, and I've forgotten the other gentleman's name. The members were all men. It was then that I was tasked to rejuvenate the organization and widen the membership to include those whom many of us knew had Japanese blood. Many were professionals, men and women.

I spent a great deal of time walking my fingers through the phone book and picking out surnames that I was sure were Japanese. I made numerous phone calls and invited everyone who claimed Japanese ancestry to a meeting. The first formal meeting took place at the International Trade Center's (ITC) 6th floor office of the Japan Consulate of Guam. The conference room was packed. Many came and listened to us talk. It was there that the seed was planted to encourage people of Japanese descent to become members of the Guam Nikkei Association. I wrote about the organization, listed names of new members, printed out information about the organization, and pasted it on foam-core boards that the group displayed as a read-through at public activities and fundraisers.

It took time for the organization, with its new members, to gain a footing in the organizational platform within the community. There was an election of a new board of directors. I was chosen to be its first president in the mid-2000s.

The Guam Nikkei Association was chartered in 2012. The organization was established with the primary purpose of perpetuating the history and lineage of those born with Japanese ancestry and who were bona fide residents of Guam. As members, they were encouraged to educate the community about the impact and contribution of the first-generation Japanese and their descendants toward the social and economic fabric of Guam and to inculcate Japanese culture, art, traditions, and history to the following generations of Japanese-Chamorro-Guamanians. The association was mandated to conduct classes, lectures, demonstrations, performances, seminars, exchange programs, travel to Japan and elsewhere, and organize community events as a means of promoting the purpose of the organization. Additionally, the Guam Nikkei Association would also seek grants and contributions, and operate fundraising activities that would provide the necessary resources to achieve the organization's purpose.

The first event was held at the Guam Premier Outlets (GPO) in Tamuneng. Monte Noda Mesa organized an exhibit of some of the members' family heirlooms, history, photos, and family trees. Twice, the group held an evening dinner event organized by David Okada at the Guam Community College cafeteria/restaurant. The paying public who patronized the event bought and ate Japanese delicacies prepared by the students enrolled in the college's culinary program.

The major highlight was the erection of a small memorial monument that listed many of the names of initial issei on Guam during the early 1900s. I painstakingly researched the list. I made the effort to contact and communicate with possible descendants to ensure that first and surnames in Japanese were spelled correctly and to let them know that their ancestors were listed on the monument. When the monument was built, I wasn't present for the unveiling. The monument was designed by the late architect Andrew Tenorio Laguana, who, himself, was married to a sansei, Joanne Sayama Shimizu of Dededo.

Another noted event, again organized by Monte Noda Mesa, was floating lighted lanterns during the evening in the waters of Ipao Beach. The project became the group's signature event every year until the COVID-19 pandemic put it on hold in 2020. The tradition was restarted in 2023. Anyone who was of Japanese lineage could join. An overwhelming response greeted the organizers, and many more individuals and families participated in the event.

The group also had a website created by Dr. Matilda Naputi Rivera, a non-Nikkei but a very good friend of mine and supporter of the organization. Dr. Rivera put together the group's website at guamnikkeiassociation. blogspot.com.

Although activities had been muted and subdued during the pandemic, in the prior years, members of the organization participated in travel and meetings with officials in Japan. Frank Ishizaki, Tommy Tanaka, Monica Okada Guzman, and Monte Noda Mesa participated in fact-finding missions and embarked on goodwill gestures of friendship, exchanges, and cultural highlights. A distinctive honor from the officials of the Japan Consulate of Guam with coordination from the Ministry of Foreign Affairs of Japan (MOFA) was recently given to Frank Shimizu, the original and long-time chair of the board of directors, the Order of the Rising Sun, Silver Rays Decoration.

Although I'm not involved in the organization anymore, there have been many programs and projects, including a youth exchange program, a martial arts exhibition, a film festival, an autumn festival, Japanese Exchange Teachers (JET), a kendama competition, and a community clean-up project.

Karl Sotto, currently serves as president; Jesse Fujikawa, as vice-president; Pauline Okada, as secretary; and Monte Noda Mesa, as treasurer.

The organization still welcomes new members at its monthly meetings.

As a final note, I have proposed to Monte Noda Mesa and Monica Okada Guzman, the possibility of having the 80th observance of Liberation Day include a memorial Mass for the unknown demise of those issei patriarchs who were never given decent burial rites toward the close of the war. Their memories should now be honored and included along with other memorials that have yearly observances such as Asinan, Assan, CHagui'an, Fenna, Manenggon, Mangilao, Tå'i, Tinta', and Fåha'.

CHAPTER 31

Relatives in Tochigi-ken
PETER

I have traveled to Tochigi-ken, specifically to the family home in Oyama City.

The first time was in 1985 when I managed an evening three-hour train ride from Tokyo. I was accompanied by my eldest daughter, Selina Maria. It was just the two of us. We arrived at our destination with help from passengers who were friendly and engaging. We were greeted by a young man whose only comment was that he "speak no English."

We followed him outside the station to a pavement path, a gravel path, through a muddy field, back to pavement, and then a smooth, but still gravel road that brought us to the family home. It was already dark. I glanced at my wristwatch and clocked our walk at exactly 15 minutes. We could barely make out the confines of the town, but, aside from the lights glaring from homes that we passed, it was, to my impression, similar to village life in Guam of the past, but, in Japan, I felt that it was a small town. Later, I was told that the town was *inaka* (backwoods country). We passed no stores, restaurants, or any type of business, and the only things we discerned were barking dogs, crickets, typical home sounds, and perhaps bullfrogs, nothing else.

At the family home, we were greeted by many ladies whose names, after introductions, I immediately forgot. There were some men, no children at all, but there were perhaps a handful of youthful-looking boys and girls who appeared to still be wearing their matching school uniforms. The young man who greeted us at the train station and walked us through the town disappeared after introductions. In his place, a college student from the town who spoke manageable English and carried a Japanese-English dictionary appeared to have been hired by the family. We, on both sides, found him useful and helpful.

Amid trays of assorted sushi, wasabi-laced sandwiches, cake and cookie desserts, and green tea, we were showered with gifts or *presento*' given to my daughter Selina Maria. I, too, brought along cans of SPAM, Spanish sausages, Tita's *guyuriha, rosketi,* shell necklaces from GVB, promotional stickers and posters of Guam, keychains, knickknacks, and miscellaneous Guam items that we passed out to those who were there. Everyone got something from us.

That evening, I was shown photo albums kept by the family. There were photos of my grandfather's early years while he still lived in the town, his father, his mother, some of his sisters, and his only brother.

In addition, there were photos of my Tåta and Nånan Dera', and my mother, her sisters, and Uncle John when they were children. I wondered who from the family in Guam had sent the photos, for they didn't know either. There were photos of my cousin Jiro', the Miss Guam Nisei that he had chaperoned and with whom I rode the float in 1960. There were letters that I wrote and forgot about to a distant cousin named Suiko. I was 11 years old at the time. I initiated those letters. Only once did Suiko write back. She wasn't there when I visited. I have never met her despite future visits. There were additional photos of family members from our side who had managed to meet them. The last of the photos were dated in the early '70s. I wish to add here that the female relatives who were present at this first meeting were first cousins to my mother and her siblings. I couldn't recall if there was a brother among them or someone who could be another male first cousin.

What was most valuable about that visit was that we all worked on a family tree. With the help of the Japanese translator/interpreter, we listed the names, surnames, and generational identities of my grandfather's sibling's children. I also contributed the names of my mother, her sisters, and my only uncle, Uncle John. I've included the family tree in this book.

Of note to me were the similar physical features between our families, most especially smiles and body frames similar to my mother, my sister, my Uncle John, and several of my cousins. It was a strong resemblance. From the sketch of that family tree that we did, I was able to let them know that by rights our last name needed to be correctly spelled to be the same as theirs, O-N-O-D-E-R-A. But legal documents and birth records on my home island of Goamu (as they called it, and for which my grandfather used when he first came to Guam), were firmly entrenched, and it would take tremendous court costs to legally correct the spelling. The women in that group explained that their surnames now reflected their married names, and ONODERA was not listed as a middle name on their birth records, including that of their children. My daughter, Selina Maria, who was with me on that first visit and is now a mother with a family of her own, decided to have her second son, Matua Ånghet, legally carry ONODERA in his middle name as his surname is Salas.

My grandfather's only surviving sister, Kimi Seki was 103 years old at that time and lived on an island in a small community in the middle of Tokyo Bay. She, according to one of the aunts, requested that I and my family, if possible, visit her. It would have involved taking a ferry to the island, and we'd have to stay there for a day or two as the ferry came every other day. We knew we couldn't chance it as Selina Maria and I were in Japan chaperoning 40 middle school students from Bishop Baumgartner Junior High School. They were on an exchange program with a public middle school that the Gyoda Jaycees sponsored in another area of the capital. And so, I never saw the last surviving elder from my grandfather's side.

One important thing that occurred on that evening was that I was given a copy of a posthumous 1968 certificate given to the family for my grandfather. It was given and signed by the Japanese Prime Minister at the time, Ojiro Ichizen. The certificate, which was translated by the Guam/Japan Consulate Office by Shizue Iriarte, was titled WHITE LOTUS MEDAL. It was presented decades after my grandfather's mysterious disappearance toward the close of World War II.

On another visit to Oyama in 2004, I was accompanied by Dr. Kayoko Nakayama, a university professor who was also the leader of a cultural dance group under Frank Rabon's guma' from På'a Taotao Tåno'. Her group's name was Guma' I Tano' yan i Tasi, for whom I wrote the lyrics of a song that is now performed as introductory dance music whenever they perform. Dr. Nakayama spoke fluent English and was learning the CHamoru language as she directed her performing arts group. Because she was Japanese and knew that I needed a translator/interpreter, she agreed to join me on that visit to Oyama City.

During the visit, I was shown a family crest, a sort of coat of arms. Then, I was taken to the Minamizumi Cemetery in Oyama City, Tochigi Prefecture. There on the family burial plot included an engraved monument honoring the memory of my grandfather. Dr. Nakayama interpreted and translated the meanings of both the family crest and the etching of the inscription on Tåtan Dera's monument.

Dr. Nakayama read: "Grandfather went to Goamu (sic), lived there, and didn't return.

The date of my grandfather's death as inscribed on the monument was August 23, 1944."

The same dates were confirmed again when I returned there in November 2023, and Hitomi, the daughter of my cousin, Motoe, from Tochigi, read and confirmed the year of death as 1944.

On the epitaph were other words engraved in *kanji* characters. I'm including the inscription along with a photo of Zenpei Jito Onodera toward the end of the book where other archival photos are shown, courtesy of the Micronesian Area Research Center (MARC) at the University of Guam and other Nikkei families. When translated, the inscription read:

Onodera, Zenpei, age 62, whose posthumous Buddhist name was Nanseiin Koun Zendo, died in the battle of Guam Island, and was a member of the 5th Naval Construction Department, commissioned by the navy. He died on August 23, 1944.

In piecing together Grandfather Zenpei Jito's life and death, he came to Guam along with contract-hire men to work at the copra plantation in the early 1900s. His birthdate was sketchy as accounts shared by Nånan Dera' and Jiro' that grandfather came to the island as a teenager, about 15 years old. This meant that his birthdate was in 1882, so he would've been 15 in 1897. Therefore, he would have already been an adult when he arrived on Guam as Tåtan Kåcha's recruit.

There's also no record as to when Tåtan Kåcha established the plantation. But the U.S. Naval government had approved his employment program, allowing him to hire a maximum of 100 overseas contract workers for a year at a time. Because the U.S. Naval Government wasn't established until the signing of the treaty ending the Spanish-American War in 1898, these types of government policies would have begun then or shortly after. It is possible that Tåtan Kåcha had already erected the buildings and facilities of both the Tokcha' and Hinapsan plantations before 1898, but his operations slowed when there weren't enough workers. Tåtan Kåcha had arrived on island by way of Saipan. By 1900, Saipan's sugar cane production was already fully operational, and Japanese nationals were already living in Saipan for about 50 years.

Because the island was liberated on July 21, 1944, Grandpa Zenpei Jito, 62, and his death date was shown on the epitaph as August 23, 1944. According to Jiro', grandfather had disappeared anywhere from June through July, during the height of intense exchange between the U. S. Marines and the Japanese. Liberation Day was on July 21, 1944, and not long after, the family was sent to live at the Tutuhan Stockade. No one knows when the information was given to grandfather's Japan family because the monument, according to Hitomi, was erected several years later, so it took time for the family in Tochigi to be given the information on Zenpei Jito's death. Further, Grandpa Zenpei Jito did not have military experience as he spent his adult life on Guam, and his refusal to be an interpreter was because of his allegiance to his CHamoru family. It must be assumed that the 5th Naval Construction Department was the entity that was tasked to record the deaths and reach families in Japan about the deaths of Japanese nationals on Guam, including that of the Japanese soldiers who perished in battle. I'll leave this matter of accuracy to the Gods as no one from the Japan side or our Guam side could prove any of these findings.

I made three more trips to Oyama City after my initial meeting with the family in 1985. I've been to Japan several other times for different activities and pursuits, but the family information for my research was my main mission. This latest update on my grandfather was a revealing one, as I had previously attempted visits to the offices of vital statistics for information where no one could help me despite being accompanied by translators/interpreters. Records dating to the early 1900s had been archived and needed to be accessed with their national database. This would require permission from a higher-up individual or individuals. My first attempt was to at least retrieve the actual birth date of Grandpa Zenpei Jito, as that information isn't included on gravestones at cemeteries, only death dates.

Fast forward to today. Thanks to Facebook, a young lady by the name of Hitomi Onodera wrote me a message, and we began writing short sentences to each other. She explained that she was 38 years old, worked at a children's park attraction, and was the youngest daughter of the man I had met in 2004. He was supposed to be an uncle, but I learned that I was older than him by a couple of years when we met. In the family tree of the Japanese ONODERA, which is also included in this book, I would place him as fourth generation. His name didn't appear on my tree because, like in Guam, I only went as far as first, second, and third generations of the families. His daughter Hitomi would be fifth generation. She was 21 years old in 2004. I didn't remember her from my visits, but she was in the photos that she sent of my daughter Selina Maria when we visited together. Hitomi was a university student at the time and must have come home to be part of the family that greeted me. She and my son Charles are the same age. The photos she sent me confirmed that I was communicating with a relative from Japan.

However, the family home that I remembered had been razed, and a new, modern two-story house stands in its place.

CHAPTER 32

Si Yu'os Ma'åse'

PETER

I'm not a war survivor. I was born after the atrocities that occurred on Guam from December 1941 to July 1944. It was horrifying that these war atrocities took place on the island where I was born and raised. It is such a contrast to what we see today on the island — the diversity, unity, and friendship among people of all nations that make the island well-known as a melting pot.

We have organizations like the first Guam Nisei Association, followed by the Guam Nikkei Association, and the Japan Club of Guam. Our island is home to folks from all the Mariana Islands, as well as many ethnicities such as Filipino, Chinese, Korean, Italian, German, Vietnamese, our Micronesian neighbors, and many others from South America, North America, and Europe. Our diversity has served to instill pride among succeeding generations of Guamanians.

I lived in San Diego for a short while and became a lifetime member of the Sons and Daughters of Guam Club of San Diego. I spoke to people from the Chamorro CHE'LU Organization, several parish church groups scattered throughout Southern California, and even a woman who traveled from Washington, D.C., and was a member of the Guam Society of America. I remembered meeting Carl Hara and his sister Patricia, both sansei from Guam, and Nan Pai', whose surname escapes me. At the time I met her, she was already a widow. Everywhere I went, I would run into other sansei, yonsei who were university students, and longtime nisei who'd been living in that part of California for decades. It was a nice experience.

Locally, I am also a lifetime member of the Young Men's League of Guam, whose origins began in 1917. Its origin was included in an early chapter as Tun Battasåt Nakasone loathed the organization because he couldn't be a member. Some of the brothers in the organization of YMLG include succeeding generations sired by the original Guam issei.

In my many travels I also met and spoke to other CHamoru and Nikkei who either once lived or still had relatives on the island. Some knew me, others remembered me, and others knew of my cousins or other distant relatives. Still, there were many who had no idea who I was. Hearing them talk about life in Guam was a wonderful thing to me. Some had good and kind memories to share, and some had negative experiences they didn't want to discuss. I considered what was told to me, truthfully, as food for thought.

Some spoke Chamoru quite fluently, and others didn't know the language. Again, I am thankful that I was able to communicate in both.

Meeting people who could not speak the language, nor had they learned Guam's traditions and customs, was in such contrast to my upbringing. I felt the influence of Nånan Dera' who babysat me while my mother worked. My earliest memories of Nånan Dera' are of her "talking story," which she related in the CHamoru language that I love so much. Although I was three years old when she died, for some reason, I remember her telling me about the *duhendes* (little people) while I pulled the *chunge'* (white hair) out of her very long tresses that she wore in a tight bundle atop her head. My mother, too, spoke fragmented English with grammar that some might consider atrocious, but I understood and loved her for that. My mother must have inherited the gift of gab from her mother for she, too, regaled me with tales of those days of her life. She talked story all the time. To me, this aspect of the culture holds importance because it's up to the individual to take the initiative to explore, ask questions, listen, watch, and learn what makes them unique from what they inherited from their ancestors and their past experiences.

I left the Guam Nikkei Association, as a dues-paying member for years, but that didn't take away my distinction as a sansei. I educated my children to know that they are yonsei, and now, too, my grandsons, who are gosei. I don't think succeeding generations after them will bother with a generational designation as the global community has become more universal and inclusive. Time may erase all these distinctions, and we will all just be Guamanians. I will probably be gone from this earth by then.

The island's Nikkei were caught between two countries and essentially left belonging to neither for a very long time. It was frightening. I wouldn't wish that on anyone.

And so, this story of the issei, the nisei, and the sansei in Guam was meant as a sort of closure. I know everyone in war is subjected to indignities — man's inhumanity to man. The reader must draw his or her own conclusions. At this writing, I don't know if there are any tomes out there that tell our story, the Nikkei on Guam. I am proud that I did this. And for the memory of those I'd interviewed and whose stories are in this book, may they rest in peace.

As a final note, when the Organic Act of Guam was signed by U.S. President Harry S. Truman and citizenship was granted to everyone on the island, the feelings of distrust, hate, and prejudice slowly started to ebb away as people became almost equal as new citizens of a nation. There are remnants of those days gone by, but they are diminishing. The continued and constant visits of Japanese tourists through the years may have also helped. Mortality rates also contributed, too, as many people who experienced the war years have now moved on to the afterlife.

Si Yu'os ma'åse' and Domo arigato gozaimasu.

MÅKPO'

PHOTO APPENDIX

Young and older photos of Jose "Katsuji" Shimizu
a.k.a. JK Shimizu and known to the pre-war
community of Nikkei as "Tåtan Kåcha."

Marianas Maru, one of the ships of Tåtan Kåcha that
traveled to and from Saipan, Guam, and Yokohama in
early 1900 and pre-war Guam. His other ship included
the Tokai Maru.

Juan "Zenpei Jito" Onodera, patriarch to the Onedera
family of pre-and-post-war Guam.

Hidesaburo Francisco Ishizaki, grandfather of former
senator Frank Ishizaki, with brothers, father, and
daughter in pre-war Tokyo.

The Guam-Japan Association of 1910-1920.

1944: Agana — A. K. Shimizu Store   ¾

Source : Sanchez Photo Collection

A post-war 1944 photo of the Hagåtña AK Shimizu Store
(from the Sanchez collection). AK Shimizu could have
been Ambrosio Shimizu, son of Tåtan Kåcha, father of
Frank S. N. Shimizu, and founder of Ambros, Inc.

A group of men comprising the membership of the
Guam Nisei Association in 1962.

Nisei, eldest daughter of the Onedera clan, and
Peter's mother Carmen Santos Onedera, at the Marbo
Laundry Facility in Andersen South, Guam.

The Onodera family crest (featured as the pattern on
the curtains in the cover art) is on gravestones of
deceased loved ones at the family cemetery in Oyama
City, Tochigi-ken.

Selina Maria and Peter Onedera with relatives on an
initial meet and greet at the family home in Oyama City,
Tochigi-ken in 1985.

Peter and Hitomi Onodera Saito, 38 years young, fourth generation Japan-side of relatives, taken in November 2023 in Tokyo.

Peter with children Selina Maria, 46; Charles Patrick, 39; Angeline Thaddea, 37; and Helen Dolores, 41.

Jose "Jiro'" Onedera, nisei/sansei with his family at his
home in Dededo. Jiro' was in his mid-70's when the
photo was taken.

The unveiling of the Guam Nikkei Association Memorial
Monument by the group officials at the War in the
Pacific Memorial Park in Yigo.

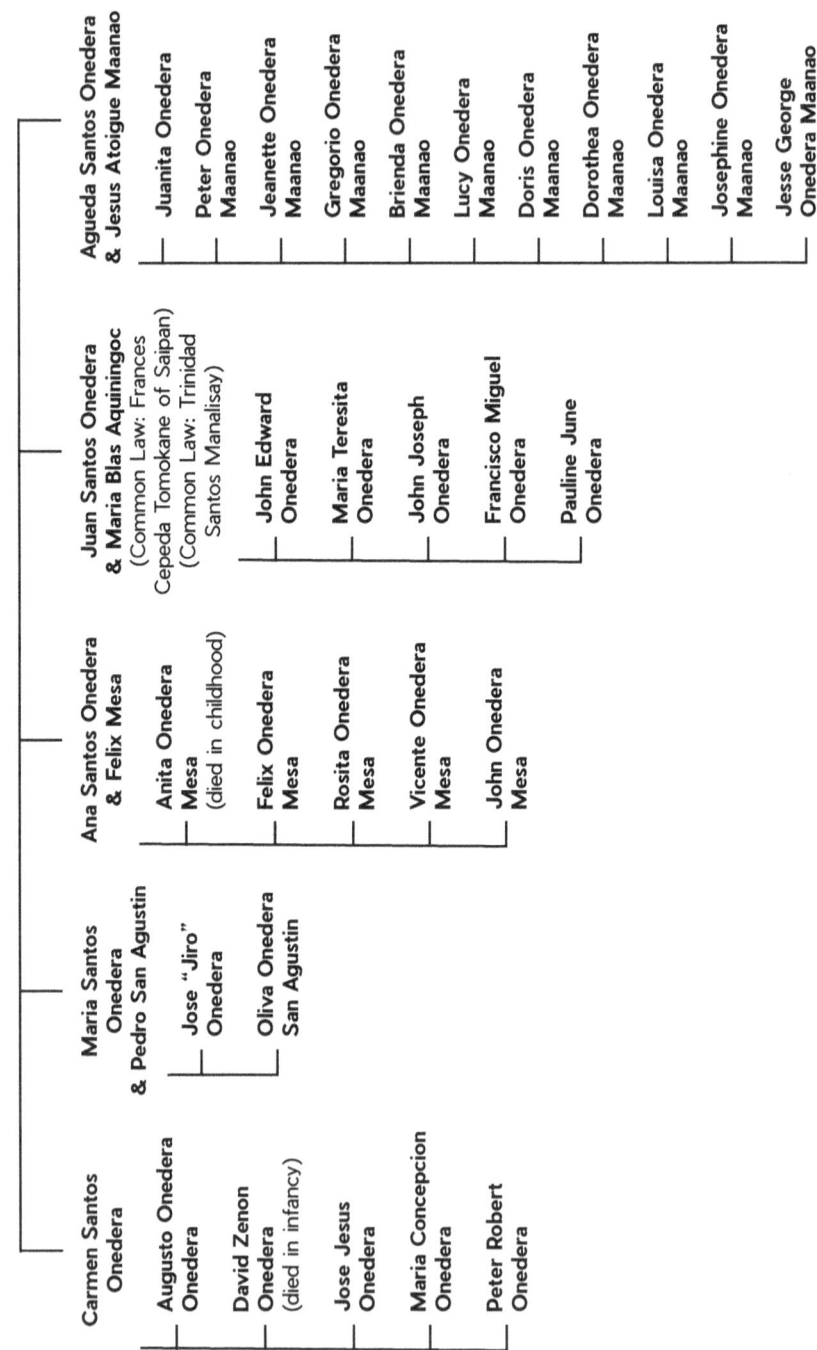

ONEDERA FAMILY TREE (*Guam*)
Maria Bae Cruz Santos & Zempei Jito "Juan" Onodera

Carmen Santos Onedera

Augusto Onedera Onedera

David Zenon Onedera (died in infancy)

Jose Jesus Onedera

Maria Concepcion Onedera

Peter Robert Onedera

Maria Santos Onedera & Pedro San Agustin

Jose "Jiro" Onedera

Oliva Onedera San Agustin

Ana Santos Onedera & Felix Mesa

Anita Onedera Mesa (died in childhood)

Felix Onedera Mesa

Rosita Onedera Mesa

Vicente Onedera Mesa

John Onedera Mesa

Juan Santos Onedera & Maria Blas Aquiningoc (Common Law: Frances Cepeda Tomokane of Saipan) (Common Law: Trinidad Santos Manalisay)

John Edward Onedera

Maria Teresita Onedera

John Joseph Onedera

Francisco Miguel Onedera

Pauline June Onedera

Agueda Santos Onedera & Jesus Atoigue Maanao

Juanita Onedera

Peter Onedera Maanao

Jeanette Onedera Maanao

Gregorio Onedera Maanao

Brienda Onedera Maanao

Lucy Onedera Maanao

Doris Onedera Maanao

Dorothea Onedera Maanao

Louisa Onedera Maanao

Josephine Onedera Maanao

Jesse George Onedera Maanao (died at childbirth)

ONODERA FAMILY TREE (*Tochigi ken, Japan*)
Hanzaburo Onodera of Tochigi married Saku Mori of Ibaraki

Zenpei Jito Onodera (son)
married Maria Cruz Bae Santos of Guam

- Carmen Santos Onedera (daughter)
- Maria Santos Onedera (daughter)
- Ana Santos Onedera (daughter)
- Juan Santos Onedera (son)
- Agueda Santos Onedera (daughter)

Kura Onodera (daughter)
married Masuji Homoriya

- Takeji Onodera Homoriya (son)
- Shiyojiro Onodera Homoriya (son)
- Risaburo Onodera Homoriya (son)
- Hankichi Onodera Homoriya (son)
- Moriji Onodera Homoriya (son)
- Tashi Onodera Homoriya (daughter)
- Kimi Onodera Homoriya (daughter)
- Moto Onodera Homoriya (daughter)

Hama Onodera (daughter)
married Kiichiro Nakajima

- Masu Onodera Nakajima (daughter)
- Junkichi Onodera Nakajima (son)
- Nakazou Onodera Nakajima (son)
- Futomi Onodera Nakajima (son)
- Suiko Onodera Nakajima (daughter)

Yasu Onodera (daughter)
married Kazuo Kimura

- Sumi Onodera Kimura (daughter)
- Haya Onodera Kimura (daughter)
- Rinichi Onodera Kimura (son)
- Teru Onodera Kimura (daughter)
- Asai Onodera Kimura (son)

Katsuji Onodera (son)
married Take Terauchi

- Hirohei Onodera (son)
- Hideko Onodera (daughter)
- Shu Onodera (daughter)
- Han Onodera (daughter)
- Hatsuko Onodera (daughter)
- Hanako Onodera (daughter)
- Keiko Onodera (daughter)

Kimi Onodera (daughter)
married Junichior Seki

- Yoshiko Onodera Seki (daughter)
- Sada Onodera Seki (daughter)
- Keiko Onodera Seki (daughter)
- Toyo Onodera Seki (daughter)
- Toshio Onodera Seki (son)

ACKNOWLEDGEMENTS

I would be remiss without first acknowledging the courageous souls of the 14 original interviewees, whom I believe most have passed away. Whether some are still living today, I've lost track. Their accounts have been presented here. Their emotions and strength at the time they were interviewed still reverberate in my mind and in my heart. These people are Maria Okada Rivera, Naoe Takano, Margaret Okiyama Martinez, Isabel Yamaguchi Gamboa, Antonio Sayama, Rosa Sudo Mesa, Magdalena Yamanaka, Sintaro Okada, Jose O. Onedera, R. Fujikawa, Jose Shiro Onedera, Artemio Fukuda, Michael Iwatso, and Winnifred Hara Torres.

I'm including others who I consulted with, spoke to, verified incidents with, and shared their own insights of what life was like. They were Jesusa F. Endo, Monica Okada Guzman, Melchoir Nakamura, Carl Hara, Rosita Mesa Tedtaotao, Jeanie O. Ellis, Felix O. Mesa, George I. Hirayama, Anthony "Malia" Ramirez, Florencia T. Palacios, Mariko C. O. Perez, Jose M. Torres, Dr. Hiro Kurashina, Dr. Rebecca Stephenson, Dr. Rosa Roberto Carter, Dr. Bernadita Camacho-Dungca, Monte Noda Mesa, Frank S. N. Shimizu, Fred Nishihira, Dr. David Shimizu, Frank Ishizaki, Tommy Tanaka, Joaquin Blas Santos, Mercedes Santos Castro, Frank BJ Agualo, Dr. Matilda Naputi Rivera, Cathy Rivera Castro, Florentina Sudo Mesa, Angie Sugiyama Paulino Mendiola, Shizue Iriarte, and my mother's goddaughter, Nan Pai', whose current Caucasian surname escapes me completely but her Japanese middle surname is one of two local Nikkei families, but I won't make the mistake of naming one without the other or both, as it would be an embarrassment.

Thanks also to others whom I've met through the years and who were able to add additional information, whether in passing, recollection, or information handed down from parents and the elderly. I spoke to many directly and some were through email. They either live somewhere in the U. S. mainland or from the various villages on the island, and, regretfully, others are now deceased. They are Carmen Iglesias Santos, Nathaniel Opena, T. F. San Nicolas, Josepha F. Trullo, Arun Villavicencio, Tomas Barcinas, Ana Borja Garcia, Rosa Salas Palomo, David Deleon Flores, Jr., Maria Ana T. Rivera, Janice San Nicolas Furukawa, Sinforosa Pablo, Manuela Pangelinan, Brienda M. Diaz, Lucy M. Barnhart, Paulne June O.B. Gozum, Doris O.M. Aguon, Maria Dela Rosa Santos, Florentinas Sudo Mesa, E. Fajardo Igemoro, Florencia T. Palacios, Nickolas San Agustin, Liz Bitanga, Father Daniel Cristobal, OFM Cap., Jesus and Concepcion Camacho Leon Guerrero, Dr. Robert A. Underwood, my elderly neighbors who knew my family-Rosa Cepeda Lizama, Juan and Catalina Pablo, Carmen Perez Vergara, Flora Baza Quan, Antonio Ojeda, Dorothy Castro Pocaigue, Arlene Borja Baza, Betsie Perez Teehan, Agnes Takano, Dorothy Imaizumi San Nicolas, Louie and Lila Gombar, and Alfred Okazaki Duenas.

For help and accompaniment to Japan to visit the Onodera, relatives include my daughter Selina Maria Onedera-Salas and Dr. Kayoko Nakayama. The others are relatives, a fourth generation ONODERA named Motoe who currently lives at the family home in Oyama City in Tochigi-ken, his daughter Hitomi and her friend Satoru Asaka. To the people who gave me the green light for final editing and eventual publication, I give my thanks to the panel of reviewers of the manuscript at the University Press, Victoria-Lola Leon Guerrero, Ralph Eurich Patacsil, Dr. Anne Perez Hattori, and Rindraty Celes Limtiaco, who did such beautiful and professional work as she edited my book.

Lastly, I was able to glean additional research information with frequent visits to the Micronesian Area Research Center (MARC) Library at the University of Guam and to my friends there, Dr. Monique Carriveau Storie, Carmen Quintanilla, Athena Meno, Jolee Bernardo, Nicolas Abrenilla, and Lourdes Tenorio Nededog (now retired); as well as through the Internet: Guampedia, Inc.; the Archdiocese of Agana church records; Antonio M. Palomo's An Island in Agony; Jose M. Torres' The Massacre at Atatte; 1920 Catholic Church Census; Guam Newsletter; Guam Recorder; Pacific Daily News; Guam Daily

News; Pacific Voice; Guam Tribune; Marianas Variety; Guam Nisei Association; the Guam Nikkei Association; Japanese Consulate Office at the Guam International Trade Center in Tamuning; Young Men's League of Guam; U.S. Naval Maritime Museum in San Diego; Yokohama Museum of Overseas Japanese Migration; and the Sons and Daughters of Guam Club of San Diego, Inc.

ABOUT THE AUTHOR

Peter R. Onedera first began writing plays that focused on issues confronting the CHamoru people. He produced and staged many of his works from one-acts, to musicals, dramas, tragedies, comedies, situational scenarios, historical accounts, and social challenges. In total, he has written 75 plays, 45 of which he produced, directed, and staged. He continues to write plays where he hopes to produce, direct, and stage again once funding, casting, and theater becomes a sought-after activity in the community. He brought his work to Saipan, Carson City, San Diego, Honolulu, and the Festival of Pacific Arts and Culture (FESTPAC) in the Solomon Islands. He has also hosted a radio talk show program titled Prugråman i Halaihai at Public Radio KPRG-FM station and wrote a column entitled CHetton Galaide' for the Pacific Daily News for several years. This bi-monthly column appeared in CHamoru in print with the English translation simultaneously published on the newspaper's website. He has written other books including Guam's Place Names for the Guam Humanities Council and two volumes of poetry – Visions of a CHamoru and Taimanu na Ini. A Borrowed Land is his endeavor at writing about his heritage as a third-generation sansei. He is also an educator, interpreter/translator, storyteller, lecturer, puppeteer, panel presenter, guest speaker, civic leader, and often referred to as an indigenous literary activist. He earned a Master's Degree in Micronesian Studies at the University of Guam after he also wrote and defended his thesis in the CHamoru language, a first for the university and for the region of Micronesia. In 2015, the Guam Council on the Arts and Humanities awarded him the distinction of Master Storyteller.

www.ingramcontent.com/pod-product-compliance
Lightning Source LLC
Chambersburg PA
CBHW020232130626
46549CB00005B/1851